D0931462

The Critical Idiom

General Editor: JOHN D. JUMP

3 Aestheticism

Aestheticism / *R. V. Johnson*

Methuen & Co Ltd

First published 1969
by Methuen & Co Ltd
11 New Fetter Lane London EC4
© *1969 R. V. Johnson*
Printed in Great Britain
by Cox & Wyman Ltd, Fakenham, Norfolk

SBN 416 14550 7 Hardback
SBN 416 14560 4 Paperback

Distributed in the U.S.A.
by Barnes & Noble Inc.

Contents

General Editor's Preface

This volume is one of a series of short studies, each dealing with a single key item, or a group of two or three key items, in our critical vocabulary. The purpose of the series differs from that served by the standard glossaries of literary terms. Many terms are adequately defined for the needs of students by the brief entries in these glossaries, and such terms will not be the subjects of studies in the present series. But there are other terms which cannot be made familiar by means of compact definitions. Students need to grow accustomed to them through simple and straightforward but reasonably full discussions of them. The purpose of this series is to provide such discussions.

Some of the terms in question refer to literary movements (e.g. 'Romanticism', 'Aestheticism', etc.), others to literary kinds (e.g. 'Comedy', 'Epic', etc.), and still others to stylistic features (e.g. 'Irony', 'The Conceit', etc.). Because of this diversity of subject-matter, no attempt has been made to impose a uniform pattern upon the studies. But all authors have tried to provide as full illustrative quotation as possible, to make reference whenever appropriate to more than one literature, and to compose their studies in such a way as to guide readers towards the short bibliographies in which they have made suggestions for further reading.

John D. Jump

University of Manchester

Introductory

'Aestheticism' means, broadly, a devotion to beauty, and to beauty primarily as found in the arts and in whatever is attractive in the world around us. (People talk of 'beauty' in other contexts – 'the beauty of holiness', for example, or the beauty of a geometrical theorem.) It might be thought that aestheticism, in this broad sense, has existed throughout civilized history. The word 'aestheticism' first appeared, however, in the nineteenth century, and it denoted something new: not merely a devotion to beauty, but a new conviction of the importance of beauty as compared with – and even in opposition to – other values. 'Aestheticism' came to stand for certain ideas about life and art – ideas which then assumed a distinct form, and presented a new and serious challenge to more traditional and conventional ideas. In England, they became recognizable in the mid-to-late Victorian period – certainly from the eighteen-sixties onwards – and in France somewhat earlier.

Aestheticism appears in different but interrelated aspects: as a view of life – the idea of treating life 'in the spirit of art'; as a view of art – 'art for art's sake'; and as a characteristic of actual works of art and literature. It was in the nineteenth century that these ideas and tendencies first clearly defined themselves, and they did so in confrontation with other ideas about life and art – a confrontation sharper, more obviously pervasive in the society and culture of the time than it is today. However, some of the ideas of nineteenth-century aestheticism are still with us; and it played an important part in the development of modern attitudes to the arts and their place in society. Thus we are partly indebted to the nineteenth-century aesthetes for the relaxation, during the present century, of literary censorship and other restrictions on literary and artistic expression.

Like other contributors to the present series, I shall be trying to explain and elucidate a term in literary criticism. Consequently, the emphasis will be on literature. Aestheticism was not, however, an exclusively literary phenomenon, although, understandably, 'aesthetic' ideas were expounded, more often than not, by men of letters, and although the implications of those ideas were, arguably, most drastic for literature. It had, however, implications for the graphic arts though not, as far as I can see, for music. (One strand in aestheticism was the desire to bring literature to a condition of 'pure art' which music was already believed to enjoy.) Also, the exponents of literary aestheticism, such as Théophile Gautier in France or Oscar Wilde in England, were interested in the other arts, and commonly spoke of 'art' and 'the artist', rather than specifically of literature.

I shall be writing for English-speaking readers and shall be mainly concerned with English literature. But any consideration of aestheticism must obviously take account of its French exponents. Aestheticism was a Western European and (if we include the important figure of Edgar Allan Poe) an American phenomenon. Writers important in the development of English aestheticism were deeply influenced by Continental writers such as Baudelaire and Gautier in France, and Hegel, as an aesthetic philosopher, in Germany. At the same time, I should hold that, notwithstanding these Continental influences, English aestheticism can still be seen as a natural development from English Romantic literature and from Romantic ideas about the creative imagination. I shall therefore stress the continuity, in England, between English Romanticism and aestheticism.

One problem, in a relatively brief treatment, is to know how far to go into the analysis of terms. 'Beauty' itself is a term that, without ungainly and futile circumlocution, cannot be avoided. In the nineteenth century the term acquired new life. 'Beauty is truth, truth beauty,' said John Keats; and the aesthetes either repeated the formula or elevated beauty above truth. But what did Keats mean?

Attempts to define or describe beauty abound. The great medieval Christian philosopher, Thomas Aquinas, defined beauty, common-sensically enough, as that which, being seen, pleases – pleases, that is, simply as an object of contemplation, whether *via* the senses or within the mind itself. The nineteenth-century French novelist, Stendhal, described beauty, in more elusive terms, as the promise of happiness (*la promesse de bonheur*) – and perhaps showed deeper insight into the feelings excited by the beautiful. Walter Pater, the foremost exponent of the aesthetic view of life, virtually refused, in the preface to *The Renaissance* (1873), to define beauty at all:

> Beauty, like all other qualities presented to human experience, is relative; and the definition of it becomes unmeaning and useless in proportion to its abstractness. To define beauty, not in the most abstract but in the most concrete terms possible, to find not its universal formula, but the formula which expresses most adequately this or that special manifestation of it, is the aim of the true student of aesthetics.

For Pater, beauty is something immediately experienced, felt upon the pulses – not a bloodless abstraction. In effect, he makes 'beauty' a blanket term covering the impressions we receive and enjoy from literature and the arts and from Wordsworth's 'mighty world of eye and ear'. This use of the word will be adopted here. While admittedly evading the philosophical issue, we shall at least be recognizing the lowest common denominator of what nineteenth-century aesthetes understood by 'beauty'; and be able at least to say where they looked for beauty and what they considered hostile to it.

Another problem arises with the word, 'aesthetic'. Here there is a danger of ambiguity. 'Aesthetic' (or 'esthetic') commonly refers simply to the beautiful (as in 'aesthetic experience' – experience of whatever strikes us as beautiful) or to aesthetics, the philosophical study of beauty and the arts. (A variant of 'aesthetics' is 'aesthetic', used as a noun, as in 'Hegel's aesthetic' – that is, Hegel's philosophy of beauty.) Aesthetics is the study of questions like: What is beauty? What is the relation of form to matter in literature and art? What do the different arts have in common? These, then, are aesthetic questions. But 'aesthetic' here has a meaning quite distinct from 'aesthetic' when it refers to the subject of this study.

When the word refers to aestheticism, it refers not merely to the beautiful, not merely to the philosophical study of the beautiful (from whatever point of view and with whatever results), but to a particular set of convictions about art and beauty and their place in life. Examples are: 'Oscar Wilde now entered his aesthetic phase'; 'Oscar Wilde is satirized, in Gilbert and Sullivan's *Patience*, as an example of the aesthetic type.' Different uses of the word are, however, very closely related and shade into each other, as in: 'He judges everything by an aesthetic standard.' There, 'aesthetic' refers to beauty as such, but also implies aestheticism, the very attitude which makes the beautiful a universal standard. To avoid ambiguity, I shall sometimes supply 'aesthetic' with inverted commas, to indicate that I am referring to the particular set of convictions known as aestheticism. Otherwise, I shall trust to the context to make the meaning clear.

Aestheticism presents questions on both the logical and historical planes. Logically, we ask about the meaning of ideas: what, for example, are we to understand by 'art for art's sake'? From a historical standpoint, we ask when ideas emerged, and under what conditions; how they resemble or differ from the ideas of earlier and later times; what motives and influences were at work in the people who conceived them; what relation they bore to life and to literary and artistic practice.

However, the two planes, logical and historical, are not completely separate. The ideas themselves are matters of historical record; they develop and change; they relate to life and to the practice of art and letters. They cannot usefully be treated completely in the abstract, like mathematical formulæ. We find that when we consider the meaning of an idea, we are concerned, not with sheer logical analysis but largely with what the idea meant to particular people – writers, artists, critics, aesthetic theorists – at particular points in history. In the case of 'art for art's sake', the idea is, logically, somewhat elusive; but we can still answer questions about its meaning for the people who defended and attacked it. We have to consider the phrase in the light of their writings or recorded utterances and of the relevant contemporary conditions. The ideas, then, must be considered in their historical context, as issuing from – and in turn influencing – the life, the inherited and contemporary culture of their time.

Some may object to the very concept of aestheticism itself: aestheticism, it may be said, is a myth, an abstraction masquerading as a concrete entity. This objection does highlight the danger of over-simplification, of imposing too tidy a pattern on the complex facts. It might be said that, in speaking of aestheticism, we are selecting writers, artists and their works, lumping them – regardless of differences – into one category, and then treating that category as if it were an entity existing apart from the individuals to whom it refers. Aestheticism would then be a 'reified abstraction', a mental concept treated as an objectively existing thing. To this objection I should reply that, as a matter of historical fact, there did exist, in the nineteenth century, a recognizable body of broadly consistent opinion to which the term, 'aestheticism' applies; that individuals did resemble each other in what they thought and said and wrote, and did make common cause together;

that with such coherence of thought and action, there did come into being a force in nineteenth-century life as recognizable as other forces – Nonconformity, for instance, Utilitarianism, Darwinism or early Socialism. In fact, without the use of such general concepts as 'aestheticism', we cannot give an adequate account of the culture of any age. Such concepts are valid in so far as they denote alignments and antagonisms formed among individuals and operating as observable forces in society and producing observable effects. There is, however, this much truth in the possible objection I have cited: we shall be considering individual writers, artists and aesthetic theorists as examples of the 'aesthetic' point of view; but the individual is likely to be more than merely an example. His achievement will present other aspects; he may not even be consistently 'aesthetic'. Even if this point cannot always be explicitly noted, it should always be remembered.

Sooner or later, in considering aestheticism, we must come to the question of its validity as an outlook on life, literature and art: we cannot maintain neutrality indefinitely. A fair assessment of the subject must evidently involve respect for facts, where facts are relevant, and, in matters of opinion, a recognition that different opinions are tenable. However, if we admit that aestheticism stands for a broadly coherent body of attitudes, both to life and art, that are still possible today, we are faced with a choice: accept or reject – or stop thinking about the relation of art and life at all. Either we accept 'aesthetic' criteria as paramount in the conduct of life, or we do not. Either we admit that art – *as* art – has its value as part of some wider scheme of values, of a total life-process that includes extra-aesthetic interests, or we do not. It is only fair, therefore, that the present writer's attitude should be made clear.

I sympathize with the nineteenth-century aesthetes' insistence, against the cruder moralists and utilitarians of the time, that art is indeed art and not something else – that the value of art is to be found in our immediate experience of it, not in its alleged effects on conduct. However, it seems to me that aestheticism, consistently followed as a comprehensive attitude to life and art, must lead to an ingrown selfishness in life and – especially perhaps in literature – to triviality in art. In the 'purer' arts of music and painting, the effects may be less deleterious. Even so, we shall find that when a serious critic of painting, Roger Fry, attempts to explain the value and significance of art, he is driven to imply some wider scheme of 'spiritual values' in which art finds its place. Art plays its role in the total economy of the human spirit; when aesthetic interests completely take over the economy, the result, as far as I can see, must be, at best, a grave limitation of personality and, at worst, a sterile, self-defeating quest for kicks.

I

Aspects of Aestheticism

In studying Victorian literature, we soon meet with references to 'art for art's sake', 'the aesthetic movement', 'aestheticism', 'the aesthetes'. We thus gather that in the later nineteenth century there appeared a body of people who distinguished themselves by the importance they attached to literature and the fine arts and to beauty generally; and that they were often regarded with disapproval by their fellow-citizens. We may see examples of Du Maurier's contemporary cartoons in *Punch*, where the aesthete figures as an affected young gentleman with long hair, velveteen jacket and knickerbockers, attended by admiring, languidly ethereal young ladies. And the name that probably most readily comes to most people's minds – if only because it has a certain facetious notoriety in modern English folk-lore – is that of Oscar Wilde.

When, however, we attempt a more precise understanding of 'aestheticism', 'art for art's sake', and related terms, the picture blurs. When we try to pin them down, the terms become oddly elusive. 'Art for art's sake' was a useful battle-cry for artists and critics claiming freedom of artistic expression; but, logically, it becomes meaningful, only if we can answer the question, 'What is art?' The aesthetic movement is, historically, a rather obscure phenomenon, since it is difficult to say of whom it ever consisted – apart from Oscar Wilde himself. (And Wilde was less important, as an originator of ideas, than his fame suggests.) Did there, in fact, ever exist anything sufficiently coherent and clearly defined to merit being called a movement at all? Again, an aesthete is often defined as somebody who appreciates beauty; but aesthetes, in this broad sense, have obviously existed before and since the nineteenth century. What was so special about 'the Aesthetes'? As for the word, 'aestheticism': this is used to denote different features of nineteenth-century culture. How do these different features relate to each other?

However, elusive as these terms may be, they have been used, since the mid-to-late nineteenth century, to denote a tendency in the literary and artistic life of the time; and that tendency was certainly not merely mythical. However vague, for instance, the formula of 'art for art's sake' may be, it meant something both to those who proclaimed it and to those who denounced it. The currency of the formula, both in France (*l'art pour l'art*) and in England, is at least evidence that many nineteenth-century people were seriously concerned with the value and nature of art, and with the relation of art to life. What was the place of art in relation to other values, such as morality and material utility? The question was not new: Sidney's *Apologie for Poetrie* (1595) defends poetry against the puritans and utilitarians of Elizabethan times. But the issue became an unprecedentedly sensitive one in the nineteenth century. There developed, in the teeth of considerable opposition, a tendency to seek in literature and the arts and in the appreciation of beauty generally, a complete answer to the individual's need for personal fulfilment, for something to give meaning to his life. Art for art's sake was one application of this general tendency, a tendency for which 'aestheticism' is the most comprehensive term.

Aestheticism was not one simple phenomenon, but a group of related phenomena, all reflecting a conviction that the enjoyment of beauty can by itself give value and meaning to life. It will be as well if I indicate now what I regard 'aestheticism' as including. Some people may prefer a wider, some a narrower use of the term than the one I shall adopt. Some might define aestheticism so

broadly as to include anybody who attached a high value to art
and the beauties of nature, independently of any views about the
importance of art and beauty in relation to other values in life.
Such a definition, I believe, would be too broad to have any
precise meaning. Writers of radically differing outlooks would be
confusingly lumped together: John Ruskin, uncompromising
moralist and public propagandist; Walter Pater, retiring and don-
nish amateur of art and philosophy; William Morris, socialist,
craftsman and man of business; and an indefinite number of others.
Of the writers just mentioned, neither Ruskin nor (in his theories
and practical enterprises) Morris is an exponent of aestheticism in
any strict and useful sense of the word. Not everybody who values
the arts and the experience of beauty would give them a paramount
and exclusive importance among human activities. John Ruskin,
for instance, was a fervent champion of what he believed to be good
in art: of the painting of J. M. W. Turner in *Modern Painters*
(1843–60), of Gothic architecture in *The Stones of Venice*
(1851–3) and other works. But art, for Ruskin, had a
distinctively moral and religious value. To put it in terms that
Plato might have used: beauty, for him, is an indispensable value
– to appreciate it is essential for the good life; but it cannot be
separated from the other values of goodness and truth, and is indeed subordinate to them. Ruskin became Slade Professor of Fine
Art at Oxford and his lectures impressed Wilde, who was later to
borrow from Ruskin as uninhibitedly as he did from other writers.
But Ruskin would not have cared to be associated with Wilde's
disparagement of moral values, of life as contrasted with art and of
truth as contrasted with beauty. The concept of aestheticism that
included both Ruskin and Wilde (or Pater or Swinburne) would
be broad to the point of nebulousness; nor would the term be
appropriate, implying, as it does, a point of view in which 'beauty'
– the aesthetic criterion – is paramount. It seems desirable, then, to
limit aestheticism so as to exclude thinkers who, while they valued

art and the beauties of nature, did not elevate them to a position of supreme – or even exclusive – importance in the conduct of life.

It is possible, on the other hand, to use the word in a narrower sense than the one I shall adopt. Aestheticism probably connotes, in many minds, the literature and art of the nineties; and it is possible to see it, with the writings and public career of Wilde and the drawings of Aubrey Beardsley in mind, as a phenomenon of the century's close, the *fin de siècle*. However, as we shall see, the term 'aestheticism' is used, in a relevant sense, from at least the eighteen-fifties. In the late sixties, Swinburne proclaims the doctrine of art for art's sake and Walter Pater the idea of treating life itself 'in the spirit of art'. 'Aestheticism' seems an appropriate term for these attitudes. Indeed, if the term be not applied to such developments of the mid-Victorian period, it is difficult to see what application – logical or historical – it could have at all. I shall try, then, to strike a middle course between a too wide and a too narrow usage.

Aestheticism can conveniently be treated in three applications: as a view of art; as a view of life; and as a practical tendency in literature and the arts (and in literary and art criticism). The first corresponds to art for art's sake; the second to what I shall call 'contemplative aestheticism' – the idea of treating experience, 'in the spirit of art', as material for aesthetic enjoyment. The third is more difficult to sum up in a phrase: for the moment it will be easier to indicate it in negative terms: a tendency, in much of the poetry and painting of the time, not merely away from moral didacticism – from any design to instruct and edify in the manner of a sermon or a moral treatise – but from any sense on the artist's part that he is called upon to speak either for or to his age at all. Not all the poets and painters who worked in the spirit of aestheticism would have subscribed to its theory. Nevertheless, creative work of the sort I have in mind is the sort an advocate of art for art's sake might be expected to approve of: 'art for art's sake' was certainly invoked in defiance of didacticism, and of any suggestion that the value of a poem consisted in its relevance to the conduct of life.

It will be convenient, in the rest of this chapter, to give a general outline of aestheticism, in the three aspects I have specified. As a view of art, aestheticism represents a drastic attempt to separate art from life. Most people would accept that art is different from life; but the aesthetic standpoint emphasizes that difference, to the point of saying that art has no reference to life, therefore no moral implications. In England this view is anticipated, early in the century, in Charles Lamb's famous essay on the Restoration dramatists: Lamb argues that the world of these dramatists is like that of a fairy-tale, that the plays do not refer to ordinary experience and that therefore we have no inclination to regard the characters' behaviour as a model for our own. Applied to all literature and art, such an attitude provides a justification of art for art's sake. France was ahead of England in the development of the concept of art for art's sake (*l'art pour l'art*), a notable exponent being the poet and novelist, Théophile Gautier, in a tendentious preface to his famous and, in its day, scandalous novel, *Mademoiselle de Maupin* (1835). Logically, the formula suffers from circularity: what, after all, is art? Two people might both profess a belief in art for its own sake, and yet mean very different things, because their conceptions of art were different. Looked at historically rather than logically, however, the formula is less opaque. We can understand the motives of those who invoked it, and what in practice, it implied. For centuries, people had generally concurred in accepting the view, attributed to the Roman poet Horace in his *Art of Poetry*, that the function of poetry (as of art generally) is to instruct and delight. (Though Horace, in one place, says 'or', not 'and' – *aut prodesse aut delectare*.) Some authorities had stressed instruction, some delight; but the dual function of literature and the fine arts was accepted, from classical times to the eighteenth century and even later, with a near-unanimity that we often forget.

One way of interpreting art for art's sake is to say that the nine-teenth-century aesthete discarded instruction, as a justification of art, and settled for delight alone. In enjoying a work of art, it was held, we enter a world that is not merely, as critics from Aristotle onwards had admitted, different from ordinary reality: it has no practically significant connection with it. A genuine work of art may contain instruction – it is rather hard, for example, to imagine a work of literature from which literally nothing could conceivably be learnt; but the instruction is merely incidental, and quite irrele-vant to its distinctive value as art. In practice, therefore, it cannot legitimately be demanded of a work of art that it convey, whether by precept or example, moral instruction or inspiration. The work is not to be valued for anything that could influence our conduct or even our general attitude to life; it is to be valued solely for the immediate aesthetic pleasure it affords. Art, as Walter Pater put it, 'comes to you proposing frankly to give nothing but the highest quality to your moments as they pass, and simply for those moments' sake'.

Aestheticism commonly attaches a high value to 'form' in art, the value of a work of art being dependent on form rather than on subject-matter. Here we enter a difficult field, in which a clear and definite use of terms is hard to achieve and it is often difficult to interpret the ideas of thinkers who were not strictly consistent. Writers like Swinburne and Pater differ from each other and, on occasion, from themselves. The only consistent feature is a high valuation of 'form' (in some sense) and a disparagement, at least relatively, of the artistic importance of subject-matter. We meet various views on the tricky question of the relation of form to matter – of where form begins and matter ends. Generally speak-ing, however, we can say that the aesthetic view of the question wavers between two possible alternatives. One is the view that form is something that can be neatly separated from matter – from, say, the subject of a poem and the attitudes it expresses – and that form, so regarded, is all that is important, as far as artistic quality is concerned.

This view assumes that there are certain formal properties – in poetry, such things as rhyme-patterns, rhythmic effects, what is now called 'verbal texture', diction, imagery – that can be appreciated entirely for themselves, independently of the thought for which they are the vehicle. It was a commonplace of eighteenth-century literary theory to regard language as 'the dress of thought', the implication being that it was the thought that was important. The extreme aesthetic position reverses the eighteenth-century maxim and represents the dress as the really important thing. The thought is merely the shop-window model on which the dress is displayed. There is one element of truth here – that, in reading a poem, we are not usually concerned with the validity or otherwise of the ideas expressed, in the way that we should be if we encountered the same ideas in, say, a philosophical treatise. (Whether this view gives a convincing account of what we *are* concerned with in reading a poem is, however, another matter.)

The other – more plausible – view is that, in our immediate experience of a work of art, form and matter are not clearly separable. It may be convenient, when talking about a work, to pick out different elements, including some under the heading of 'form', others under the heading of 'matter'. But in our immediate response, form and matter merge in the total impression it makes upon us. When I read and enjoy a poem, I cannot say: this part of my experience I owe to the thought, and that part to the language, imagery, rhythm in which it is conveyed. Our total experience of a poem is indivisible: even though some elements may be highlighted and others in shadow, they still affect us in conjunction with each other. Can we clearly distinguish, for example, between the purely nervous, physiological effect of a particular verse-rhythm and the more complex, emotive effect which results from the conjunction of the rhythm with the sentiments expressed? To take a conveniently simple example from Flecker's *War Song of the Saracens*:

> We are they who come faster than fate:
> we are they who ride early or late:
> We storm at your ivory gate: Pale Kings
> of the Sunset, Beware!

The effect of the warlike sentiments and the effect of the insistent metrical and rhyme pattern are inseparable from each other. The same metre used in another context – say, a humorous one – would have quite a different effect. 'Form' and 'matter' act upon each other. It was this experiential unity of works of art that inspired Walter Pater's famous dictum that all art aspires to the condition of music, in which, he held, form and matter are indistinguishable. Swinburne, on the other hand, sometimes wrote as if form and matter were distinct entities, form, as he understood it, being all that counts. However, both Pater and Swinburne were pleading for the autonomy of art against those who would estimate a poem, painting or sculpture simply by the philosophical or moral sound-ness of the sentiments it expressed. (By such a criterion, a Victorian puritan could have denounced Marvell's poem, *To His Coy Mistress*, as an incitement to sexual licence.) Pater does not dispute the supremacy of form; but he seems to hold, on occasion at least, that 'form' is not something separable from matter, but precisely the total unity into which matter is absorbed, and in relation to which (not to any external canons, moral, religious or otherwise) it acquires a distinctively aesthetic value.

Underlying such views on form and matter is the assumption that literature, music and the graphic arts have enough in common for generalizations about 'art' in general to apply to all of them in particular – that they are, in fact, all forms of the one thing: art. This assumption is still quite common. It is worth mentioning, however, because it fostered, in the nineteenth century, an ideal of 'pure art' (and 'the pure artist') which had important effects on ideas about literature. Literature is, arguably, impure art – as an art critic of the present century, Clive Bell has maintained – because it is dependent, unlike music and to a far greater degree than the graphic arts, on ideas; it thus often tends to aspire, not to the condition of music (Pater's ideally pure art) but to that of non-artistic discourse. Thus the novelist may deviate into the role of psychologist; the religious poet into that of theologian. It may be held, however, that literature should emulate the 'purer' arts. The keen interest of such men as Swinburne and Pater in painting and sculpture probably encouraged them to regard a work of literature as an art-object, closely comparable with work in other media. Another instance of this tendency is the novelist, George Moore's notion of 'pure poetry' – poetry which conveys no more comment on life than a Ming vase. This ideal of a poem as pure art-object is far from dead in the present century: it is implied, for instance, in the maxim of an American poet, Archibald MacLeish, that 'a poem should not mean but be'.

Another way of interpreting art for art's sake, then, is to see it as an attempt to regard all artistic expression in the same way that we may regard music and non-representational graphic art – ceramics, purely decorative designs or the abstract painting and sculpture of the twentieth century. Thus, in literature, the writer will try to evoke the same pure aesthetic response that is evoked by a vase or a fine piece of jewellery. The logical tendency of art for art's sake – whether anyone actually follows it out or not – is, on this interpretation, not merely away from moral didacticism, from any comment on life, but away from meaning as such. This is, of course, an extreme interpretation but it follows logically enough from the idea that art is totally separate from life. The ideal it postulates is not strictly possible in literature; but, if meaning cannot be eliminated, it can still be diluted to a point at which we are no longer sharply conscious of it. And some Victorian poetry, as I shall indicate later, does move in this direction.

The idea of literature as 'pure art' represents the completest repudiation of the demand that it convey some improving message. At a less advanced – and only marginally 'aesthetic' – stage, art for art's sake could mean simply a plea for the artist's freedom (and even responsibility) to express only what he has it in him to express. He should not be swayed either by other people's expectations or even by his own convictions, if these tempt him into merely propagandist or didactic exposition. The artist must learn to distinguish between what, at least for him, is suitable for artistic expression and what is not. Thus Pater praises Keats and Lamb as exemplars of 'the love of art for its own sake'. They confined themselves to what they had it in them to express in literary form, whereas the other Romantic writers, such as Wordsworth and Shelley, deviated into political and philosophical concerns that were artistically intractable and also of merely ephemeral interest. Here again there is an element of truth: writers cannot always give effective literary statement to everything they have at heart: strong political conviction, for example, is not always accompanied, even in poets of genius, by the ability to write good political poetry. In so far as art for art's sake enjoins the artist to be true to his own special but limited gift, it has practical point; though at the same time it could conceivably deter him from genuinely extending his scope. How is a writer to be sure of the limitations of his powers other than by trying to extend their range – as Keats, after all, was doing to the end of his career? In fact, remarks such as Pater's, cited above, were scarcely calculated to encourage any writer with a strong interest in expressing political, religious or philosophical ideas.

Art for art's sake may, finally, be seen from two sides – the artist's or his audience's. It may refer to the lack of any need for an ulterior intention, to edify or instruct, on the artist's part – even to the undesirability of such an intention; or it may refer to the lack of any desire to be edified or instructed on the reader's (viewer's or hearer's) part. Generally, it probably refers to both; though such exponents as Swinburne and Gautier may be supposed to have been primarily concerned with the writer's problems. Either way, the concept again contains elements of truth: it is probably true that the artist is rarely much concerned, in the heat of composition, with anything but the immediate matter in hand; and it is also true that an earnest desire to be edified is not the most promising frame of mind in which to approach a work of art. It does not follow, however, that the work of art may not embody and communicate insights into life, and be valued because of them.

*   *   *

To turn from aestheticism as a view of art to aestheticism as a view of life: this implies taking life 'in the spirit of art', as something to be appreciated for its beauty, its variety, its dramatic spectacle. The classic statement of this view in English is the concluding essay in Walter Pater's *The Renaissance*, a collection of essays on art and literature first published in one volume in 1873. To pursue the aesthetic life, as Pater describes it, we must cultivate our whole area of awareness, sharpening intelligence, sense-perception and powers of introspection. Pater was accused of advocating selfishness and sensuality. The first charge had some truth in it, the second was less just. He advocated the cultivation of a varied sensibility, not unreflecting self-abandonment or the unbalanced concentration on one area of experience only. However, Pater's aestheticism could easily fall foul of any rigid moral prohibitions; and it was genuinely opposed to the spirit of puritan morality. Hostile critics of *The Renaissance* were right to recognize something subversive of commonly received standards.

I take the 'puritan morality' mentioned above (or what is sometimes nowadays called 'the protestant ethic') to be a code of behaviour, deriving from the Puritanism of the sixteenth and seventeenth centuries, and stressing industry, temperance, useful activity. The good life, in this view, is essentially active; life is a moral struggle, represented metaphorically as a pilgrimage (as in Bunyan's *Pilgrim's Progress*) or a battle. This puritan ethic was generally accepted in the largely Nonconformist middle class that was increasingly setting the public tone of Victorian society. By contrast, the aesthetic viewpoint involved detachment, an avoidance of wholehearted involvement in practical affairs. The aesthete aspires to treat life, not as a battle but as a spectacle. As so often, it is a French writer, here Villiers de l'Isle-Adam, who, through the hero of *Axel* (1890), expresses the viewpoint with the most resounding effect: 'Live? Our servants will do that for us.' Only by detachment can the aesthete 'appreciate' life as a spectator; he is the spectator even of his own emotions. (This, presumably, involves the difficulty of being simultaneously inside and outside his own skin.) The aesthetic approach to life is thus contemplative, not active. I shall use the term 'contemplative aestheticism' both to stress this point, and to distinguish aestheticism as a view of life from art for art's sake, which is largely a statement of policy to be followed by active practitioners of art.

In the conclusion of *The Renaissance* Pater conveys a world-weary scepticism. We seek reality and find, in the world about us, only change, a constant succession of phenomena. Turning inwards, we find that our own consciousness is equally fugitive, a drift of momentary sensations and thoughts. We cannot be sure of any enduring reality behind the flow of phenomena; we cannot be sure that we ourselves have any stable identity. The world is constantly slipping away, and we with it. What, then, can we do but make the most of experience as it passes?

> While all melts under our feet, we may well grasp at any exquisite passion, or any contribution to knowledge that seems by a lifted

horizon to set the spirit free for a moment, or any stirring of the senses, strange dyes, strange colours and curious odours, or work of the artist's hands, or the face of one's friend.

We are certain of one thing only: death. 'We are all under the sentence of death but with a sort of indefinite reprieve.' Let us, then, make the most of life while we have it.

Practically, much depends on what we think is the best way of making the most of life. For Pater, all depends on 'a quickened, multiplied consciousness', an experience that is at once intense and varied. Anything in the nature of repetition – including, one would think, the compulsive behaviour of the vulgar sensualist – is to be minimized. 'In a sense it might even be said that our failure is to form habits; for, after all, habit is relative to a stereotyped world, and meantime it is only the roughness of the eye that makes any two persons, things, situations seem alike.' How, then, are we to maintain such alert sensitivity? Pater does not positively prescribe any single way; and his interests were wider than his reputation as the high priest of English aestheticism might suggest. Thus he commends the study of philosophy; but, significantly, he does not commend it as a means of arriving at truth – 'truth' is unattainable – but because it highlights features of experience. (Thus a study of the problem of free-will and determinism may not yield an answer; but it will heighten our awareness of the human condition, of which 'freedom' and 'determinism' represent different aspects.) 'Philosophical theories or ideas, as points of view, instruments of criticism, may help us to gather up what might otherwise pass unregarded by us.' This, however, is a rather limited endorsement of philosophy. And it is art that, for Pater, adds most to our experience:

> Of such wisdom, the poetic passion, the desire of beauty, the love of art for its own sake, has most. For art comes to you, proposing frankly to give nothing but the highest quality to your moments as they pass, and simply for those moments' sake.

Here the reference to 'the love of art for its own sake' has fairly clear implications: art is to be valued for the immediate impression it affords, for something received at the moment of appreciation, not for any purely hypothetical after-effects. This is in keeping with his earlier remark: 'not the fruit of experience but experience itself is the end.'

While contemplative aestheticism may commend a rich and varied experience, it may also prompt a retreat from life – from what most people, pressed by circumstances, involved in personal relationships and engaged in definite occupations, would regard as life. It obviously presupposes leisure and a freedom from humdrum pressures. The supreme exemplar of the aesthetic retreat from ordinary life is, perhaps, Des Esseintes, the hero of the French novel by J. K. Huysmans, *A Rebours* (*In Reverse*, 1884). Des Esseintes shuts himself in his room, and, with the aid of various stimuli, including medieval ecclesiastical objects and the novels of Dickens, seeks to objectify the private world of his imagination. Once, he is sufficiently stirred by his enthusiasm for Dickens to start on a journey to London; however, he sees so much of English tourists and their habits in Paris that he decides he has seen enough of England to enhance his appreciation of Dickens, and returns home.

Contemplative aestheticism can, however, assume more positive moral implications than it does in the conclusion of *The Renaissance*. The appreciation of life involves the appreciation of people and, if this is more than superficial, an enhanced understanding of them. Thus Pater pleads elsewhere for a morality of sympathy, one that dissolves hard and inflexible moral rules and estimates people with due regard to circumstances and individual temperament. Here again aestheticism diverges from a puritan ethic of rigid 'thou shalt nots'.

Contemplative aestheticism reflects a common Victorian aspiration after personal culture – 'self-culture' as it was sometimes called.

In the conclusion of *The Renaissance*, the ideal of self-culture receives an extreme statement. For Pater, the cultivation of sensibility is not merely a desirable thing; it is the only thing that can make sense of life, and, ideally, embraces the whole of it.

To burn always with this hard, gemlike flame, to maintain this ecstasy, is success in life.

This is hardly a conventional concept of success. Like Matthew Arnold, in *Culture and Anarchy* (1869) and elsewhere, Pater deplores the pre-occupation with what Arnold called 'machinery', the attitude which envisages life in terms of means and ends; so that in practice, everything tends to become only a means to something else; personal fulfilment is put off till tomorrow, which never comes. People, as Pater remarks in an essay on Wordsworth, become 'like thorns in their anxiety to bear grapes'. In his attack on such short-sighted 'practicality', Pater is with Arnold, though without Arnold's social awareness: he writes for a few kindred spirits. None the less, we can recognize the point of his challenging maxim: 'not the fruit of experience but experience itself is the end' – that it is possible to become pre-occupied with the means of living, to the neglect of living itself.

* * *

The third aspect of aestheticism – as a practical tendency in literature and art, and in literary and art criticism – has so far only been indicated negatively, as a movement away from didacticism, from any pretension to convey a moral or to expound a philosophy of life. This tendency can be seen as corresponding to the principle of art for art's sake; and, like the principle, the practice, at its extreme limit, strains away from meaning itself, towards something like the 'pure poetry' envisaged by George Moore. Relevant developments are: a movement, in both poetry and painting, away from contemporary life into realms of antique, exotic or pastoral fantasy; the depiction, especially in poetry, of states of mind that were, in terms of commonly accepted standards and taboos, either suspect in themselves or too intimate for public display; a high valuation of sensuous – particularly visual – imagery and description; and a certain suppression or vagueness of subject-matter. This last effect was achieved, in poetry, by subordinating the precise use of language to the quasi-musical evocation of mood, and by highlighting stylistic and formal devices, not merely as appropriate to the matter in hand, but as intriguing in themselves.

All these developments are at least consonant with the spirit of art for art's sake, as understood at the time; and all of them are apparent in those poets, such as D. G. Rossetti and Swinburne, who were most closely associated with aestheticism. But we obviously cannot assume that any poet who exemplifies such characteristics was committed to 'aesthetic' ideas; and not all the developments in question have any necessary connection with such ideas. For instance, the expression of suspect states of mind could obviously be prompted by motives quite unconnected with aestheticism: one Victorian poet, whose partiality for off-beat characters and emotions needs no labouring, is Robert Browning, and Browning's philosophy was certainly not 'aesthetic'. On the other hand, another development – the elevation of musical or pictorial values in poetry, above precise thought or the clear delineation of the subject – is one that finds its most obvious justification in aesthetic concepts of 'pure art'.

The connection between theory and practice can, therefore, easily be oversimplified. However, 'aesthetic' theories were not conceived in isolation from what was actually being done in contemporary literature and art; often the theorizing was designed to explain and justify the practice. Both the theories and the practical developments bear witness to a divergence of the artist from the mainstream of contemporary life and thought. This divergence was not universal: it is evident, for instance, in poetry rather than in the novel; in the early Tennyson, more than in the Tennyson of *Idylls of the King*; in the paintings of Burne-Jones, not in those of Landseer or the later Millais. But, if not universal, the divergence was noticeable enough to provoke widespread contemporary comment and complaint.

Here I shall cite one contemporary comment which is both illuminating in itself and of special interest as containing a very early use of the word, 'aestheticism'. In an essay, 'Alfred Tennyson's Poems', published in 1855, George Brimley comments: '*The Lotus-Eaters* carries Tennyson's tendency to pure aestheticism to an extreme point. It is picture and music, and nothing more.' Here, in the mid-fifties, we already find a concept of literary aestheticism that is consistent with the one I am trying to outline here. In fact, the critique of *The Lotos-Eaters* is worth quoting at length:

> If music and picture – the feelings of imaginary beings, in a pure reign of imagination, perfectly presented in rhythmical language that takes the formative impulse of the feeling, as falling water does of the forces that draw it into a flashing curve – have no charm for any mind, that mind can find no interest in *The Lotus-Eaters*. To attempt to treat it as an allegory ... to read it as we should read *The Pilgrim's Progress* and look for facts of actual experience that answer to its images, is as monstrous and perverse as it would be to test a proposition of geometry by its rhythm and imagery. A mood of feeling, of course, it represents, and feeling dependent on, and directed to distinct objects, – in this latter respect, alone, differing from music. We may, of course, too, apply the mood of feeling thus depicted to the real events of life. ... So we might with a sonata of Beethoven's, – but the application is ours, and not the composer's.

(*Cambridge Essays, contributed by Members of the University*, London, 1855, p. 237)

Tennyson, Brimley claims, is inspired by 'a purely musical impulse'; and his poem 'does not ... belong to the region of articulate speech'. Here, a couple of decades before Walter Pater, an English critic presses the analogy between poetry and music, commending a poem for its musical quality. Brimley admits that even poetry such as this must refer, unlike music, to 'distinct objects'; but these objects belong to the 'pure reign of imagination' – the poet is not inviting comparison between the world of his poem and actual life. Here, too, we find a recognition of the intimate unity of matter and form – of feeling with its sensuous expression – as characteristic of a poetry that aspires to the condition of music: feeling shapes language as the force of gravity does a waterfall. And there is the insistence that poetry need not be valued for its ideas, or for any application to life.

Perhaps Brimley overstates his case: it is not difficult, especially in the light of other poems by Tennyson, to relate the world-weary scepticism of *The Lotos-Eaters* to the poet's religious anxieties. However, the poem does not refer directly to contemporary religious and philosophical issues, as do other poems, such as *The Two Voices* and *In Memoriam*; it is the evocation of mood that finally counts. Most of us will read the poem in the spirit that Brimley did:

> There is sweet music here that softer falls
> Than petals from blown roses on the grass,
> Or night-dews on still waters between walls
> Of shadowy granite in a gleaming pass;
> Music that gentlier on the spirit lies,
> Than tired eyelids upon tired eyes.

These lines can be described in pretty much the terms Brimley uses: 'picture and music, and nothing more'. That Tennyson himself sometimes thought in terms of the analogy between poetry and music, is evidenced in an earlier lyric, *Claribel*. This is merely a juvenile exercise; but it illustrates the tendency under discussion. A few lines will suffice:

Where Claribel low-lieth
The breezes pause and die,
   Letting the rose-leaves fall:
But the solemn oak-tree sigheth,
   Thick-leaved, ambrosial,
With an ancient melody
Of an inward agony,
Where Claribel low-lieth.

Claribel is significantly subtitled *A Melody*. The motive behind this subtitle is comparable to that behind the title given by James McNeill Whistler to his famous painting of his mother, exhibited in 1872: *Arrangement in Grey and Black*. Whistler presumably wanted people to appreciate the painting as a purely aesthetic composition, not for its human interest. In Tennyson's poem the actual subject is thinned down almost to vanishing point. We barely gather that a girl has died and that the narrator is mourning her. Claribel herself is quite overwhelmed in the flow of musically and (for Tennyson) rather vaguely evoked sights and sounds.

In *The Lotos-Eaters*, 'picture and music' become the almost self-sufficient carriers of mood. The poem is based on a brief episode in Homer's *Odyssey*, when some of Odysseus's crew land on an island and succumb to a narcotic fruit given them by the islanders. This episode provides little more than anchorage for a mood that constantly tends to cut adrift into something like the 'suppression or vagueness of mere subject' that Walter Pater was to regard as the condition of musical quality in poetry. Not all nineteenth-century critics, however, were sympathetic to this tendency: 'music' involves a sacrifice of intellectual substance that some regarded as too great. Thus, one critic in *The Quarterly Review* referred to 'the splendid but meaningless music of Mr Swinburne'. Tennyson, in *The Lotos-Eaters*, retains a strong respect for natural phenomena and at least his pictures are clearly

c

drawn. Swinburne later carries musicality to a point at which references to natural phenomena are studiously vague:

> When the hounds of spring are on winter's traces,
>   The mother of months in meadow or plain
> Fills the shadows and windy places
>   With lisp of leaves and ripple of rain.

F. R. Leavis's comment is apt: 'We are not to visualize the hounds of spring, or to ask in what form winter is to be seen or conceived as flying or whether the traces are footprints in the snow, or snow and frost on the grass: the general sense of triumphant chase is enough.' We can say, keeping Brimley's terms, that here 'music' has taken precedence even over 'picture'. How we judge such poetry depends on our presuppositions about what poetry should be and do. Leavis believes that literature should foster an intelligent openness to the possibilities of life: hence he naturally objects to Swinburne's invitation to suppress our intelligence and sensuous alertness. A critic who expected only a pleasurable aesthetic impression might regard Swinburne's method as a legitimate means to that end. Others, including the present writer, might concede that Swinburne achieves a distinctive and memorable effect, while preferring a poetry that more fully engages and extends our awareness.

Another way in which Victorian poetry tended to establish itself in a separate realm of its own was through archaism, whether in style or in subject-matter. The fact that a poet writes in an archaizing style about persons and events in a remote – and, probably, largely imaginary – past does not in itself imply that his work will lack application to contemporary life. Spenser's *Faerie Queene*, for example, is full of contemporary, Elizabethan references; and Tennyson, in *Idylls of the King*, uses Arthurian legend to exemplify Victorian ideals. However, it remains true that the past – particularly its literature and legend – can provide materials for a fantasy-world, in which poet and reader can escape from the uncongenial present. Some Victorian poetry virtually creates such a separate world by the 'literariness' of its inspiration. Thus William Morris, in *The Life and Death of Jason*, retells a classical legend in a quasi-Chaucerian style; the poem is thereby set at two removes from the modern world. More subtly, Dante Gabriel Rossetti, in *The Blessed Damozel*, drawing on Dante and other, more elusive sources, creates a Heaven that is neither Christian nor pagan – that is not related, in fact, to any specific scheme of life on earth:

> The blessed damozel leaned out
> From the gold bar of Heaven;
> Her eyes were deeper than the depth
> Of waters stilled at even;
> She had three lilies in her hand,
> And the stars in her hair were seven.

The properties, including the mystical numbers, three and seven, are vaguely medieval; but the damosel, with her piquant blend of sexiness and sanctity, is not the sort of person one would expect to meet in the Christian Heaven. Rossetti's Heaven, indeed, is suspended in a philosophical vacuum; the effect is, consequently, dreamlike and misty. The poet has, with a judicious vagueness, evoked a miniature cosmos of his own: nothing that happens in it relates to the world we know, and the poem, memorable as it is, remains closed upon itself.

The escape into archaism also appears in a certain formalism – in Rossetti's elaboration of the ballad refrain, for example:

> Heavenborn Helen, Sparta's queen,
>   (*O Troy Town!*)
> Had two breasts of heavenly sheen,
> The sun and moon of the heart's desire:
> All Love's lordship lay between.
>   (*O Troy's down,*
>   *Tall Troy's on fire!*)

Among lesser poets, especially in the nineties, there was a taste for old verse-forms, such as the sixteenth-century French villanelle, a poem of six stanzas, with line repetitions and only two rhymes throughout. An instance is Oscar Wilde's *Theocritus*, of which I give the first three stanzas:

> O singer of Persephone!
>   In the dim meadows desolate
> Dost though remember Sicily?
>
> Still through the ivy flits the bee
>   Where Amaryllis lies in state;
> O singer of Persephone!
>
> Simætha calls on Hecate
>   And hears the wild dogs at the gate;
> Dost thou remember Sicily?

Such a verse-form is not resurrected by poets seeking a suitable vehicle for some matter they urgently desire to express; in general, it springs from, and appeals to, a taste for evident formal dexterity and for rhyme-patterns that strike insistently on the ear. It is not, perhaps, surprising that one practitioner, W. E. Henley, should have written a villanelle *on* this verse-form, beginning 'A dainty thing's the villanelle'. The elevation of 'form', considered as something separable from matter, could not go much further. Admittedly, the partiality for such a verse-form itself reflects a mood of the time – a certain flippancy which becomes particularly marked in the nineties and which can take a comic or a wistful turn.

The cult of 'form' implies a repudiation of the demand for serious import in literature. In some poets we also find a more overt flouting of conventional expectations – in the treatment of 'dangerous' subject-matter; or in the expression of conventionally unacceptable sentiments. Contemporary reactions to this tendency included Robert Buchanan's 'The Fleshly School of Poetry' (1871), attacking the sensuality in Rossetti, and reviewers' protests against the feverish sexual fantasy of Swinburne's *Poems and Ballads* (1866). Browning and even Tennyson were occasionally rebuked for indelicacy. The limitations conventionally imposed on literary expression were most stringent where sex was concerned; but they extended beyond it. Tennyson, for example, originally withheld one poem, *Tithonus*, from publication because its world-weary pessimism was insufficiently tonic for the temper of the time. A writer did not, of course, have to be 'aesthetic' in outlook to want to flout current taboos; but the desire for freer expression was one motive behind the plea of art for art's sake. (Witness Wilde's assertion that no book can be branded as immoral: there are only well written books and badly written ones.) When we think of the moralistic protests evoked by novels such as George Moore's *Esther Waters* (1894), Thomas Hardy's *Jude the Obscure* (1896) and, in France, Flaubert's *Madame Bovary* (1856), we can at least recognize that nineteenth-century aesthetes had a genuine battle to fight, whatever we may think of the ground on which they chose to fight it.

Naturally enough, aestheticism had its implications for criticism, as well as for literature and the arts themselves. On the more extreme interpretation of art for art's sake, ethical, religious and philosophical criteria have no relevance to the value of a work of art: content is important, if at all, only as it enters into a total aesthetic impression. The critic's task is, therefore, to enable other people to receive the impression that a given work has the power to afford them. (It is assumed, reasonably enough, that there may be difficulties in achieving good reception; the critic seeks to cut out interference.) The result is 'impressionistic' or 'appreciative' criticism. (A collection of critical essays by Walter Pater, the best known English exponent of this type of criticism, is actually entitled *Appreciations*.) In the preface to *The Renaissance*, Pater expounds his concept of the critic:

The aesthetic critic [meaning here simply the literary or art critic] . . . regards all the objects with which he has to do . . . as powers or forces producing pleasurable sensations, each of a more or less peculiar or unique kind. . . . [His function] is to distinguish, to analyse, and separate from its adjuncts, the virtue by which a picture, a landscape, a fair personality in life or in a book, produces this special impression of beauty or pleasure, to indicate what the source of that impression is, and under what conditions it is experienced.

In practice, Pater seeks to re-create, in the reader's mind, the pleasurable impression a work makes on himself, relating this to recognizable features of the work. He points out, for example, a certain sadness in the expression of Botticelli's Madonnas, and then asks: why do these unusually mournful Madonnas appeal to us?

At first . . . you may have thought there was something in them mean or abject even, for the abstract lines of the face have little nobleness, and the colour is wan. For with Botticelli she too, though she holds in her hands the 'Desire of all nations', is one of those who are neither for Jehovah nor for His enemies; and her choice is on her face. The white light on it is cast up hard and cheerless from below, as when snow lies upon the ground, and the children look up with surprise at the strange whiteness of the ceiling. Her trouble is in the very caress of the mysterious child.

It will at least be apparent from this detached example that Pater, when he wishes to re-create the impression that Botticelli's Madonnas have made on him, resorts to literary artistry himself. How otherwise, after all, could he re-create an aesthetic impression as actually felt? Criticism thus approximates to the condition of art. It is not surprising that Wilde, Pater's professed disciple in criticism, should have written an essay, *The Critic as Artist* (1890).

Impressionistic criticism is exposed to certain hazards. Impressions differ: the critic may point to objective features but the same features may affect another person in a different way. In *The Critic as Artist*, Wilde actually argues that the critic need only regard the work as a stimulus to fantasy: a piece of good criticism is a work of art in its own right – it does not have to tell us anything about its ostensible subject. The impressionist critic does not, in fact, have to write in the way Wilde recommends; and it is not only the impressionist critic who risks falling into subjectivism. However, there is certainly a danger of stressing the impression at the expense of the work itself. And where do we draw a line between impression and objective source? Where, in Pater's comments on Botticelli's Madonnas, does mere observation of detail end and critical interpretation begin? In practice, we can only measure the critic's impressions against the work itself; and, fortunately, even an interpretation that we cannot wholly accept may still draw our attention to features we had not hitherto noticed.

Pater, in the preface to *The Renaissance*, does not include judgement among the critic's tasks: he is to *interpret* works of art, not to say whether they are good or bad. Criticism is 'appreciative', rather than evaluative. It is not particularly surprising that aestheticism should foster critical appreciation – the expression and communication of enjoyment – rather than judgement. If all we can ask of a work of art is that it should affect us, in Pater's phrase, 'with a special, a unique, impression of pleasure', there will probably be few works, above a minimal level of competence, that will not offer at least something of interest. And if all we want is pleasure, however 'special' its quality, there seems little reason to bother with works that do not provide it: they are best ignored. Those, at the other extreme, who consider that art has a part to play in the formation of our whole response to life, will take more seriously the task of identifying those works which are equal to such a function. One of the critic's major tasks will be to separate the wheat from the chaff. In fact, we will generally find that a strong emphasis on critical evaluation goes with a strong moral conviction: this applies, in the nineteenth century, to Matthew Arnold, who argues, in 'The Study of Poetry', that poetry is destined to encroach on the traditional role of religion in fostering ideals; and that we should therefore become more exacting in our poetic standards. A comparable attitude appears later in the criticism of F. R. Leavis. It is true, of course, that we may have strong moral convictions without stressing the moral function of literature as much as these critics would.

The confrontation between utilitarian moralists and aesthetes tended to obscure differences between members of the 'aesthetic' camp. Thus we find 'art for art's sake' covering two different views of art: the formalist – regarding 'form' as the sole essential value in art – and the expressive. The latter view amounts to an assertion of the artist's right and responsibility to express what he has it in him to express, to be true to his own talent, not to the expectations of 'society'. This position is virtually a moral one – an assertion of personal integrity. Also, in emphasizing what the artist expresses – his attitude to the matter he presents – it exposes itself to extra-aesthetic contagion. Thus, when Walter Pater, in an essay on 'Style', expounds an expressive theory of literary style, he finally concedes a distinction between 'good art' and 'great art', great art being distinguished by its presentation of matters of major human import. Pater's divergence from strict aestheticism reminds us that original writers rarely conform consistently to a generalized concept of aestheticism, or of anything else.

The aesthetes, again, were limited by the very puritan morality they combated. There need not be an exclusive choice between a moralistic, utilitarian view of art and an 'aesthetic' view of art as separate from all ethical considerations. To experience *King Lear* is to feel – not just intellectually recognize – the terrible contrasts of the human condition, the reality of goodness, together with its vulnerability. This experience is elevating in itself, apart from any effects it may – or may not – have on conduct. It raises, if only for a time, our quality as human beings.

2

The Emergence of Aestheticism

In the Victorian age itself, aestheticism was seen as originating in the Romantic period. An anonymous critic in *The Quarterly Review* of January 1876 referred to Walter Pater as 'the most thoroughly representative critic that the romantic school has yet produced'. 'Aesthetic' symptoms do occur early. In 1831, we find Arthur Hallam proclaiming, in a review of his friend Tennyson's poems, that the poet should concern himself with sensuous beauty to the exclusion of other considerations:

> Whenever the mind of the artist suffers itself to be occupied, during its period of creation, by any other preoccupation than the desire of beauty, the result is false in art.

Hallam here looks forward to Poe, Baudelaire and Swinburne. Later, conservative critics, such as those of *The Quarterly*, were to see writers such as Pater, Swinburne, Rossetti as exemplifying an individualism in taste and sentiment, a disregard of generally accepted standards, that had pervaded literature from Wordsworth onwards.

The Romantics had extolled imagination, both as a means of insight into the world and as the power which governed poetic composition. For Coleridge, imagination was the 'shaping spirit': a poem derives unity from the imaginative vision which pervades it, not from conformity to external rules: a poem resembles not a machine constructed to a blueprint but a living creature organized within by its own vital principle. Again the imagination is essentially an active power: it modifies all it touches. In the same spirit,

Wordsworth talks of giving to objects 'a certain colouring of the imagination'. The effect of Romantic ideas of imagination was to discredit rigid rules – those of a declining neo-classicism – and any narrow naturalism or 'realism'. A poem was regarded as an autonomous creation, the world of poetry as different from – if related to – the real world.

This shift in literary principles emphasized the difference between literature and ordinary life, and the freedom and self-sufficiency of the poet who enjoys a special vision to which alone he is responsible. There was a tendency, in the post-Romantic generations, to see the poet as a phenomenally sensitive soul alienated from the general life of his time. This tendency was encouraged, probably, by the guttering of radical political hopes. The extension of the franchise to the middle class in 1832 did not produce the sweeping improvements in society that its more idealistic advocates had hoped for: John Morley, politician and man of letters, remarked in 1874 that the prosaic results of political reform had 'damped the wing of political fancy. The old aspirations have vanished, and no new ones have taken their place'. Shelley saw the poet as the prophet of change; the aesthetes found their inspiration in Keats, 'the pure and serene artist', as Wilde was to call him. (Though Swinburne preferred the revolutionary Shelley.) Tennyson gave expression, in an early poem, to the post-Romantic conception of the superiority of the poet to common mortals, and of imagination to more humdrum modes of thought:

> Vex not thou the poet's mind
>   With thy shallow wit:
> Vex not thou the poet's mind;
>   For thou canst not fathom it.

In unsympathetic minds, this post-Romantic attitude fostered the familiar cartoonist's image of the poet – a long-haired, effeminate dreamer drooling over skylarks and daffodils. The more sympathetic view was not always vastly different. (Witness the poet in

Shaw's *Candida*.) Not only the Philistines represented the poet as ineffectual in ordinary life: Baudelaire compares the poet to an albatross, a bird clumsy and ludicrous on the deck of a ship, but graceful and masterful in the sky.

Comparable and closely parallel to this conception – of the poet as different from other mortals – is the new conception of 'the artist'. Significantly, the artist – in the sense of one who works in *any* of the creative arts – was virtually a nineteenth-century invention. Previously, 'artist' commonly meant either someone versed in 'the liberal arts' – a person of learning and general culture – or someone with a special skill, 'creative' or otherwise. The word could comprehend people as various as poets, painters, doctors, stonemasons and astronomers. In the nineteenth century, however, creative artists were commonly thought of as in a class apart, and 'artist' acquired a special and frequently honorific sense. This use of the word indicates that, for a significant number of people, creative artists had come to acquire a special status, implying a new concept of the artist's relation to society.

Another word which acquired a new sense in the nineteenth century is 'Bohemian'. The artist or otherwise aesthetically minded person could now live in a subculture of artistic nonconformity. The landmark here is Henri Murger's *Scènes de la vie de Bohème* (*Scenes of Bohemian Life*, 1845–49). The growth of Bohemia, from the coffee-houses of the eighteenth century onwards, is related to the decline of a system of aristocratic patronage and the rise of the modern literary and artistic market. The effects of this change are hard to sum up: the artist became less of a hired performer in aristocratic households; on the other hand, the successful artist had had a recognized place under aristocratic patronage, even if it was not vastly different from that of a cabinet-maker. In the nineteenth century, the artist often felt out of place in a commercially orientated society; and the middle class came to be represented, in a term Matthew Arnold was to popularize in

England, as 'the Philistines', the moralistic and money-grubbing corruptors or opponents of aesthetic values. In these circumstances, the artist became, as for Stephen in James Joyce's *Portrait of the Artist* (1916), a myth by which people aspired to live.

As early as 1863, a writer in *The Saturday Review* complains:

> Young people no longer break their hearts for love; but they fancy that they are born to be artists, and quarrel with the trammels of society or business, with the frigid round of conventionalities and the monotonous occupations that tie the wings of their Pegasus.
>
> ('Aesthetical Delusions', XV, 138)

Society is considered to be at fault if it does not indulge the aspiring artist's vagaries:

> It follows that mere sensibility is substituted for morality. Whatever seems to the artistic spirit good and beautiful, that he is bound to pursue, or to sell his birthright.

Regarding life merely as material for art, the artist devoted himself to a quest for novel sensations:

> He fosters peculiar emotions in order to observe their progress and conclusion. He does strange things, like Firmilian, to get a strange sensation.

Here the leading elements of aestheticism are already present, ten years before the publication of Pater's *Renaissance*.

In the aesthetic outlook, Romantic ideas were pushed in the direction of greater subjectivity, of withdrawal from actual life. The Romantic – virtually Coleridgean – view of imagination appears, for instance, in an essay by Pater on the German eighteenth century writer, Winckelmann:

> The basis of all artistic genius lies in the power of conceiving humanity in a new and striking way, of putting a happy world of its own creation in place of the meaner world of our common days, generating around itself an atmosphere with a novel power of refraction,

selecting, transforming, recombining the images it transmits, according to the choice of the imaginative intellect.

There is nothing here that Coleridge had not anticipated; nor, in substance, do Pater's remarks imply more than Coleridge – or even Philip Sidney in Elizabethan times – had said about the idealizing tendency of poetry. The phrasing might, however, suggest that art merely offers escape from 'the meaner world of our common days'. (This is a view we shall meet in Wilde's essays.) The emphasis on the power of imagination could also suggest that imagination can render anything artistically acceptable, however wicked or repulsive it might commonly be considered. Thus Swinburne praises Baudelaire for his ability to 'give beauty to the form, expression to the feeling, most horrible and most obscure to the senses or souls of lesser men'. This raises another possible implication of 'art for art's sake' – that art constitutes a segregated world of its own, to which ordinary values are quite irrelevant.

The fact that literature and the arts do not give us merely a replica of actual life has been recognized since Aristotle, whose concept of poetry as imitation (*mimesis*) has often been misunderstood. Aristotle recognized that the poet selects from the facts of experience, keeping only those which are relevant to his purpose. He presents some general truth, stripped of the accidental circumstances that obscure it in actual life. Thus Aristotle argues that, although (or because) poetry is not a mechanical repetition of life, it may convey general truth. The poet gives us an ordered vision, not a mere 'slice of life'; but it is a vision in which some aspect of experience is heightened and illuminated. Where the aesthetic standpoint differs is in stressing the difference between art and life, while ignoring or denying the capacity of art to give particular embodiment to general truth. The realm of imagination is not merely different from actuality: it does not refer back to it in any way. We value a poem, play or novel, not because of its ordered rendering of truth but precisely *because* it constitutes a fictive world other – even better – than the actual world.

* * *

The movement of thought and sensibility that fostered contemplative aestheticism is reflected in a poem by Matthew Arnold, *The New Sirens* (1849). There he evokes the temptations offered by 'the new sirens' of Romanticism. The temptation is to a life of intense and passionate experience as something valuable in itself. In a world where belief is disintegrating and intellect seems to exercise only a negative and destructive function, why not seek fulfilment in – what alone we can be sure of – the life of feeling?

> 'Come,' you say, 'opinion trembles,
> Judgement shifts, convictions go:
> Life dries up, the heart dissembles:
> Only, what we feel, we know.
> Hath your wisdom known emotions?
> Will it weep our burning tears?
> Hath it drunk of our love-potions
> Crowning moments with the weight of years?'

The argument here anticipates the conclusion of Pater's *Renaissance*: we are sure of nothing but immediate experience – so let us make the most of that. Like Pater, Arnold's new sirens offer a counsel of despair – one which Arnold himself rejects. Pessimism provided, in some Victorian minds, a strong inducement to seek satisfaction in the here-and-now, the classic expression of this mood in Victorian literature being Edward FitzGerald's *Rubáiyát* of Omar Khayyám. Where Omar Khayyám sought consolation in

> a Loaf of Bread beneath the Bough,
> A Flask of Wine, a Book of Verse – and Thou,

the devotees of aesthetic 'self-culture' sought it in the pleasures of the mind, particularly of literature and the arts and the beauties of the world around us.

Self-culture was not merely a cult of despair: it represented also a positive – and characteristically Victorian – aspiration to a better mode of life. It also represented a revulsion against materialism and insensitivity. Arnold saw England as threatened by a tide of narrow moralism, vulgar materialism and parochial complacency. His 'Culture' was offered as an antidote to these diseases of the national life, diseases that, in his mind, were closely connected with the increasing influence of the middle class on the nation as a whole. Arnold's Culture was more socially orientated than aesthetic self-culture; but the influence of Arnold on Pater and Wilde was a real one. Aestheticism belonged to a wider revulsion against certain features of Victorian society – against vulgar materialism, with its elevation of (in modern terms) gross national product as the criterion of civilization; against the toleration of ugliness; against the utilitarian spirit which disparaged intellectual pursuits; against the puritan moralism which conceived the good life solely in terms of 'doing good', in a material sense, and avoiding evil – in a sense which some held to be narrow and arbitrary.

An interesting account of 'Culture' appears in a satire, *The New Republic* (1877), by a minor Victorian prophet, W. H. Mallock. Mallock caricatures Pater as 'Mr Rose, the Pre-Raphaelite'; but another, more sympathetically conceived character, Laurence, interprets 'Culture' in terms that are very close to the conclusion of *The Renaissance*:

> A person is really cultivated when he can taste not only the broad flavours of life – gulping its joys and sorrows down, either with a vulgar grimace of disgust, or an equally vulgar hearty voracity; but *when with a delicate self-possession he appreciates all the subtler taste of things*, when he discriminates between joy and joy, between sorrow and sorrow, between love and love, between career and career; discerning in all incidents and emotions their beauty, their pathos, their absurdity, or their tragedy as the case may be.

The affinity with Pater is perhaps most striking in the words I have italicized. In fact, neither Pater nor Mallock was breaking completely new ground: earlier, in *The Gay Science* (1866), E. S. Dallas had commented caustically on 'the life of culture'.

> The example of Goethe has had a prodigious effect on the more highly educated minds among us – teaching them *to value self-culture above all things* [my italics], and to indulge a selfish appetite for more and more experience . . . We all know how to despise the vices of solitary indulgence – say, solitary drinking; and it is something more than a jest to say that solitary thinking is akin to solitary drinking. Then again, we smile at the vanity of the girl who is always at her mirror, who watches there the play of her pretty features, and whom, perhaps, we catch kissing herself in the glass. But what is her vanity to the self-love of the man who is always looking at his own mind, studying it in all its phases and attitudes, pampering it here with the memory of an old experience, touching it there with the rouge of a new sensation, and treating it ever as a picture which is to have another and another charm added to it?

Dallas's charges – selfishness, narcissistic vanity and effeminacy – are representative of contemporary attacks on 'self-culture'. The condition which Dallas deplores as a form of psychological self-abuse, is accepted by Pater in *The Renaissance*, without misgiving: he declares that 'the demand of the intellect is to feel itself alive', and speaks of the modern consciousness as 'brooding with delight over itself'. Wilde was later, with a characteristic touch of flippancy, to make the same point: 'we watch ourselves, and the mere wonder of the spectacle enthralls us'. Here, as so often, the preoccupations of late-Victorian aesthetes were anticipated in France: the Chevalier d'Albert, the hero of Gautier's *Mademoiselle de Maupin*, confesses: 'Too much, I listen to myself living and thinking: I hear the pounding of my arteries, the pulsations of my heart.' (*Je m'écoute trop vivre et penser: j'entends le battement de mes artères, les pulsations de mon coeur.*)

*　　　*　　　*

In trying to relate aestheticism to the main currents in Romantic and post-Romantic culture, we must consider Pre-Raphaelitism, a movement with which, since the Victorian age itself, it has often been associated.

Pre-Raphaelitism began as a quite clearly defined phenomenon with the foundation, towards the close of the eighteen-forties, of the Pre-Raphaelite Brotherhood. This was a group of people, not exclusively painters but devoted primarily to recovering English painting from the academic conventionality to which they believed it had succumbed. 'Pre-Raphaelite' referred originally to their disparagement of Raphael's influence and that of high Renaissance painting generally: they aspired instead to the truth and simplicity of Giotto and other medieval painters. The best-remembered of the P.R.B., as it came to be called, are the painters, Holman Hunt and John Millais, and the poet and painter, D. G. Rossetti.

Originally, then, Pre-Raphaelitism was a movement with fairly definite and limited aims. Aestheticism, by contrast, was scarcely a 'movement' at all, but rather a broad tendency, apparent in individuals who often shared no more than a general affinity in taste and ideas. The Pre-Raphaelites, however, maintained tight solidarity, signing their paintings with P.R.B. after their names, and promulgating their views in a short-lived journal, *The Germ* (January–April, 1850).

Tight as the group was, however, its members differed widely in temperament. Holman Hunt, the future historian of the group, was devoutly religious, and painted with a definite aim to edify and instruct. (His *Light of the World* belongs to popular religious art.) In *The Germ* itself we find religiously inspired essays such as John Seward's 'The Purpose and Tendency of Early Italian Art'. Significantly, John Ruskin supported Pre-Raphaelitism, recognizing a spirit akin to his own in the group's concern for visual truth as something morally incumbent on the painter. Among early Pre-Raphaelite attitudes, we find hatred of sensuality – 'a

D

meanness', as Seward describes it, 'repugnant to youth and
disgusting in age'. Voluptuousness, he declares, is the infallible
sign of deterioration in art. (Other signs are 'exaggerated action,
conventionalism, gaudy colour, false sentiment . . . poverty of
invention'.)

The Pre-Raphaelites believed that the impulse that gave birth
to established forms had spent itself, and that characteristics once
genuinely expressive had hardened into conventional gestures.
Despite the achievements of Constable and Turner, eighteenth-
century conventions still prevailed in the academic painting of the
mid-nineteenth century – a circumstance to which Ruskin's pro-
test in *Modern Painters* bears witness, as do Holman Hunt's
reminiscences. However, although Pre-Raphaelitism was a movement of artistic revolt, it was not revolutionary in any wider sense.
Rather, its dominant aim was to reclaim art as a medium for fostering truth, piety and virtue, as traditional Christianity conceived
them.

Not all Pre-Raphaelites, however, wholly shared the prevailing
ethos – certainly not Dante Gabriel Rossetti, whose deviations are
sadly recalled by Hunt. Like Hunt and Millais, he painted religious
subjects, such as the childhood of Mary; but in a different spirit:

> Rossetti treated the Gospel history simply as a storehouse of interest-
> ing situations and beautiful personages for the artist's pencil, just as
> the Arthurian legends afterwards were to him, and in due course to
> his later proselytes at Oxford.
>
> (*Pre-Raphaelitism and the Pre-
> Raphaelite Brotherhood*, 2 vols., Lon-
> don, 1905, I, p. 172)

Here Hunt refers to a later phase in Pre-Raphaelitism, in which
Rossetti was associated with William Morris and the painter,
Edward Burne-Jones. Hunt himself shrank from subjects which
offended piety; but Rossetti was guided solely by 'loyalty to the
supremacy of genius, and perfection in art'. Rossetti was not much

given to theorizing; but he did write a short prose narrative, 'Hand and Soul', the story of a fictitious painter, Chiaro dell'Erma, who, to convert his fellow-citizens from their violent feuding, paints an allegory of peace. One day, Chiaro sees his painting literally spattered with the blood of combatants; afterwards, he is told in a vision to consult his own heart and paint only what he finds there. Rossetti's fable clearly tells against didacticism and in favour of the artist's exclusive loyalty to his personal vision.

From the mid-fifties, Rossetti strongly influenced Morris and Burne-Jones; the latter's dreamily suggestive treatments of Arthurian and other medieval or legendary themes contrast with the moralism and prosaic detail of Hunt and the early Millais. From the first, Rossetti's own paintings and poems body forth a private world of sensuous fantasy. Pre-Raphaelitism can thus be seen in two phases, the second of which was more favourable to aestheticism. Of the original Pre-Raphaelites, it was Rossetti who commanded most influence over the tastes and attitudes of a later generation.

Later Pre-Raphaelitism fostered tastes in art, domestic decoration and dress that became prevalent in intellectual and artistic circles. Mrs Humphry Ward, the novelist, recounts how she and her Oxford friends of the seventies furnished their houses with 'Morris papers, old chests and blue pots', and dressed in a style modelled on the paintings of Burne-Jones – 'Liberty stuffs very plain in line, but elaborately smocked' and 'evening dresses, "cut square" or with "Watteau pleats".' The taste is that affected by the aesthetes in Du Maurier's *Punch* cartoons. In attributing Pre-Raphaelite tastes to contemporary aesthetes, Du Maurier may have been drawing on actual observation; but he was also, in effect, smearing people like Mrs Ward who, whatever their tastes, were certainly not aesthetes.

*　　　*　　　*

Who, in fact, *were* the aesthetes ? In what sense did there ever exist an aesthetic 'movement' at all ? It was in the late seventies and early eighties that, to judge by printed comment, aestheticism was most in the public eye. Satire against the aesthetes began sporadically in the seventies, and reached its peak in Du Maurier's cartoons and in two highly successful stage productions of 1881, Gilbert and Sullivan's *Patience* and F. C. Burnand's farce, *The Colonel*. This was also the period of Oscar Wilde's first impact on London society; and it is Wilde who figures in *Patience*, as Bunthorne, 'a fleshly poet'. (1881 also saw the publication of Wilde's *Poems*.) In 1882, Walter Hamilton published his book, *The Aesthetic Movement in England*. Hamilton credits the eminent journalist, George Augustus Sala, with the gibe that the aesthetic movement was merely a fiction concocted by popular lampoon-writers and cartoonists. This attractive theory represents something of an over-statement; but it is probable that the satirists would have had a much harder job if they had not had the bizarre figure of Wilde as a focus for ridicule, and if they had not, somewhat unfairly, represented Pre-Raphaelite tastes as evidence of 'aesthetic' attitudes. The effect of contemporary satire is to make aestheticism seem a tightly coherent movement, which, in contrast to early Pre-Raphaelitism, it was not. There was, for instance, no such close association between Pater and Swinburne, in the late sixties and early seventies, as there had been between Hunt, Millais and Rossetti about 1850; nor did any group as dedicated and as clearly orientated as the P.R.B. gather round Wilde in the early eighties. Aestheticism is recognizable as a current of taste and ideas, as a 'tendency' rather than a 'movement' – even though the latter word was already applied to it in the eighteen-eighties.

Pre-Raphaelitism had itself become a more widely diffused, more indefinite phenomenon: 'Pre-Raphaelite' became a smear-word, virtually interchangeable with 'aesthetic'. The movement had always included writers as well as graphic artists; and parallels naturally presented themselves between the literary work of Rossetti and Morris and their work in painting and decorative art. Hence, 'Pre-Raphaelite' came to embrace literature as well, and this wider use survives: Swinburne, Rossetti and Morris are often classed together as Pre-Raphaelite poets.

Another term which calls for comment is 'decadence' or 'the Decadence'. This is an elusive term, inevitably implying personal value-judgements. We can recognize easily enough the ostentatiously deviant strain in Swinburne's *Dolores*:

> Cold eyelids that hide like a jewel
> Hard eyes that grow soft for an hour;
> The heavy white limbs and the cruel
> Red mouth like a venomous flower.

As we have seen, Swinburne praised Baudelaire for his ability to give artistic form to subjects and sentiments that most people found repellent. It may be argued that this represents a natural development of Romantic ideas about imagination, especially when those ideas are divorced from the moral, social and religious convictions of a Wordsworth, Coleridge or Shelley: the liberated imagination, seeking the new and strange, finds it in conventionally suspect areas of feeling. Also, there is no doubt that aestheticism appealed to deviant temperaments: the homosexuality of Wilde is the notorious instance. It could also be argued that contemplative aestheticism, in its quest for stimulus, must strain beyond the frontiers of conventional feeling: those who live for kicks, however refinedly and sophisticatedly, will take their kicks where they find them.

'The Decadence' often denotes the nineties – a much-maligned decade! – and, among other phenomena of the period, the drawings of Aubrey Beardsley (1872–98). Beardsley is now enjoying a revival: the taste of the mid-twentieth century has tended towards the 'sick' and the kinky, in some of its serious art as well as in light entertainment; and these elements are evidently present in the grotesqueries of Beardsley. A cool and consummately skilful draftsman, he gave enduring expression to the 'decadent' mood. By comparison, the earlier, poetic deviations of Swinburne seem dated and rather absurdly hectic.

'The Decadence' also often refers to the lives, as well as the work, of some poets and artists who flourished – if that is the word – in the nineties. Wilde is the best known instance; but other literary figures of the time, such as the poets, Ernest Dowson and Lionel Johnson, showed a comparable leaning towards squalor and disaster, illustrating in their lives the nineteenth-century French concept of 'the cursèd poet' (*le poète maudit*). This concept, apart from its factual basis, is a natural enough development of the post-Romantic tendency to see the poet as a misfit: poverty, debauchery – 'low life' generally – almost constitute his native element.

The link between aestheticism and decadence is perhaps a matter for speculation. It may be that aestheticism, like vulgar hedonism, comes up against the law of diminishing returns – that beauty, like happiness, evades us when too persistently and self-consciously pursued, and that the lover of beauty is, sooner or later, impelled to seek it in things not commonly considered beautiful. Symptoms of decadence were observed quite early by Victorian critics: as we have seen, *The Saturday Review* commented, in 1863, on the artistic type who 'fosters peculiar emotions'. Ten years later the *Saturday* still represented the aesthete in a comparable light:

> 'Life,' he tells an adoring group, 'is not action but art; and art is the delirious contemplation of the infinitely little' . . . The beauty he loves is the beauty that springs from decay – the poetry of Baudelaire, the bronzes of Pekin, the faded graces of Madame de Pompadour.
>
> ('Art in the Home', XXXVI, 1873, 777)

Perhaps for the aesthete, absorbed in his own impressions, beauty is even more in the eye of the beholder than it is for most of us.

He may become like the hero of *Mademoiselle de Maupin*, who declares:

> I should not be astonished if, after offering up so many sighs to the moon, staring so often at the stars, and composing so many elegies and sentimental apostrophes, I were to fall in love with some vulgar prostitute or some ugly old woman. That would be a fine downfall! Reality will perhaps revenge herself in this way for the carelessness with which I have courted her.

(Trans. Burton Roscoe, New York, 1929, p. 92)

3
Aestheticism and
Poetry: Poe to Moore

The literary implications of aestheticism were brought out most clearly in connection with poetry. The first important exponent of 'aesthetic' views of poetry, in English – and, also, perhaps, the most original – is the American poet, short story-writer and literary theorist, Edgar Allan Poe (1809–49). Poe is best known for his *Tales of Mystery and Imagination* and for a few poems, such as *Annabel Lee* and *The Raven*; but his ideas on poetry were influential beyond the English-speaking world. He was greatly admired by two major French poets of the nineteenth century, Charles Baudelaire (1821–67) and Stéphane Mallarmé (1842–98). Baudelaire translated the *Tales* into French; and the influence of Poe's ideas on poetry is apparent in his *Notes Nouvelles sur Edgar Poe* and other essays. Baudelaire's own ideas in turn influenced his English devotee, Swinburne.

Poe's ideas, stated mainly in two essays, *The Philosophy of Composition* (1846) and *The Poetic Principle* (published posthumously in 1850) anticipate art for art's sake and the idea of 'pure poetry'. In *The Poetic Principle*, he attacks 'the heresy of the didactic' – a phrase rendered into French by Baudelaire as '*l'hérésie de l'enseignement*', and thence restored to English by Swinburne as 'the great didactic heresy'.

> It has been assumed, tacitly and avowedly, directly and indirectly, that the ultimate object of all Poetry is Truth. Every poem, it is said, should inculcate a moral; and by this moral is the poetical merit of a work to be adjudged. We Americans especially have patronized this

happy idea; and we Bostonians, very especially, have developed it in full. We have taken it into our heads that to write *a poem simply for the poem's sake* [italics mine] and to acknowledge such to have been our design, would be to confess ourselves radically wanting in the true Poetic dignity and force:– but the simple fact is that . . . there neither exists nor *can* exist any work more thoroughly dignified – more supremely noble than this very poem – this poem *per se* – this poem which is a poem and nothing more – this poem written solely for the poem's sake.

Poe sees poetry and truth as incompatible. He distinguishes sharply between poetic utterance and scientific and philosophical statement.

The demands of Truth are severe. She has no sympathy with the myrtles. All *that* which is so indispensable in Song, is precisely all *that* with which *she* has nothing whatever to do. . . . In enforcing a truth, we need severity rather than efflorescence of language. We must be simple, precise, terse. We must be cool, calm, unimpassioned. In a word, we must be in that mood which, as nearly as possible, is the exact converse of the poetical.

'Truth', for Poe, is apparently truth of fact and logic; it does not comprehend truth of feeling. Poetic language is not merely irrelevant to truth; it obscures it.

Poe divides the human mind into 'Pure Intellect, Taste and the Moral Sense'. The three have common ground in our nature, but their 'offices' or functions are different. They concern themselves with different members of the Platonic trinity of values: Intellect with Truth; Taste with Beauty; and the Moral Sense with Goodness (Duty). Taste may concern itself with Duty, but with Duty only in its aesthetic aspect: it may be drawn to the beauty of virtue and recoil from the ugliness of vice. It follows that poetry may contain 'the precepts of Duty; or even the lessons of Truth'; but they must serve the true end of poetry, which is the excitement of the soul in the contemplation of Beauty. This position, in fact, seems to allow for didacticism – provided the poet is didactic in the right way. This could imply merely that the moral import (if any) of a poem reaches us in a different way from that of a sermon or ethical treatise. If so, most of us would agree; but Poe seems to imply, beyond this, that moral import in poetry cannot be more than incidental. Quite rightly, he rejects the moralistic fallacy which consists in saying: this work is morally sound – *therefore* it is good literature.

In *The Poetic Principle*, Poe does not define Beauty. He believes that life on this side of the grave gives us only partial intimations of it. The thirst for Beauty 'belongs to the immortality of Man. It is at once a consequence and an indication of his perennial existence'. The poet who merely enthuses over 'the sights, and sounds, and colours and sentiments, which greet him in common with all mankind', is thus falling short of Poe's ideal: rather, he should excite a sense of Beauty beyond the beauties experienced in this life.

> And thus when by Poetry – or when by Music, the most entrancing of the Poetic moods – we find ourselves melted into tears – we weep them . . . through a certain petulant, impatient sorrow at our inability to grasp *now*, wholly, here on earth, at once and for ever, those divine and rapturous joys, of which *through* the poem, or *through* the music, we attain to brief and indeterminate glimpses.

Poe speaks of the thirst for Beauty in Shelley's phrase – 'the desire of the moth for the star'. The beauties of this world are only dim shadows of 'the Beauty above', and therefore our enjoyment of them is tinged with sorrow and frustration. In *The Philosophy of Composition*, he declares: 'Beauty of whatever kind, in its supreme development, invariably excites the sensitive soul to tears. Melancholy is thus the most legitimate of all the poetic tones.' This sentiment is certainly not peculiar to Poe: the association of beauty with melancholy is fairly constant in nineteenth-century lovers of beauty from Keats onwards.

It is impossible here adequately to consider Poe's elusive but

interesting concept of beauty – bound up as it is with his unorthodox ideas on immortality. (I refer the curious reader to his *Eureka:
an Essay on the Material and Spiritual Universe.*) The soul is aware
of possibilities of beauty beyond what the present life affords.
This 'Beauty above' is not, however, a Platonic, absolute beauty:
Poe's theory, when he comes, in *The Philosophy of Composition*, to
speak more specifically of beauty as it appears in poetry, is sub-
jectivist. Beauty is an effect, and, as such, inseparable from the
mind which experiences it:

> When, indeed, men speak of Beauty, they mean, precisely, not a
> quality, as is supposed, but an effect – they refer, in short, just to that
> intense and pure elevation of *soul* – not of intellect, or of heart – upon
> which I have commented, and which is experienced in consequence
> of contemplating 'the beautiful'.

Beauty, it seems, is – or cannot exist apart from – an 'excitement,
or pleasurable elevation of soul'. We infer that Poe's 'Beauty
above' is not above the soul but above the soul's present capacities.
Beauty is something experienced in moments of intense 'elevation'; and this concept of the intense aesthetic moment is vital to
Poe's theory of poetry.

In both the essays under consideration, Poe argues that a long
poem is an impossibility: the phrase, 'long poem', is a contradic-
tion in terms. Poe's argument virtually equates poetry with the
short lyric. In this and in his high estimate of the musical element in
poetry, Poe anticipates the views, in England, of Pater and George
Moore.

A poem, Poe maintains, *is* a poem by virtue of its capacity to
afford us 'elevating excitement'; excitement, however, is
momentary, and cannot be sustained through a long composition;
therefore, a 'long poem' can, at best, only be a sequence of good
passages – in effect, short poems – linked by stretches of dead
writing. (We may admit that most long poems – including *Paradise
Lost* or even Dante's *Divine Comedy* – are unequal in quality.)

For Poe, a poem succeeds through 'the impression it makes . . . the effect it produces' – meaning the *immediate* impression or effect, at a given point of time. He explicitly denies that a poem's total effect may be built up by the relatively dull passages as well as by the more exciting ones. 'The ultimate, aggregate, or absolute effect of even the best epic under the sun, is a nullity.' Poetry is experienced as an aesthetic moment, not as an idea which the mind gradually takes in. This view accords with his opinion that poetry addresses itself to sensibility ('Taste') rather than to intellect: poetry is something *felt*, and felt intensely. Obviously, we form an idea of the total action of *Paradise Lost* as we read, and may derive pleasure from watching the action unfold; but this has nothing to do with poetic effect – if we define poetry, as Poe does, in terms of sustained intensity of response.

Poe's view of poetry contrasts with that advanced by Matthew Arnold a few years later. In 1853, Arnold published a volume of poems, with a preface attacking contemporary tendencies in poetry. Poets, says Arnold, seem now to pursue vivid words and images before anything else, and to value impressive lines and passages more than the total effect of a poem. Here Keats has been a particularly bad influence: *Endymion* is so incoherent it scarcely merits being called a poem at all, despite its incidental flashes; while *Isabella*, though 'a perfect treasure-house of graceful and felicitous words and images', is so loosely constructed, 'that the effect produced by it, in and for itself is absolutely nil'. Arnold, speaking with reference to narrative and dramatic poetry, urges modern poets to emulate the Greeks who always regarded the whole and made the details contribute to a coherent scheme. The subject of the poem should take precedence over brilliance of diction and imagery. In his emphasis on design, construction, architectonic quality, Arnold differs from Poe: no amount of 'elevating excitement' will compensate for a deficiency in that 'ultimate, aggregate, or absolute effect' which for Poe was a nullity

and for Arnold was supremely important. Arnold represents a
'classical' reaction in nineteenth-century taste; Poe, with his sub-
jectivist view of poetic 'Beauty' and his conception of poetry as
intense, momentary excitement, represents a late-Romantic standpoint, anticipating the aesthetes.

Both in theory and practice, Poe upheld a 'musical' view of
poetry that gathered strength in England, and in France. (*De la
musique avant toute chose*, enjoined the Symbolist poet, Paul
Verlaine (1844–96): 'music before everything else'.) 'Music', in
connection with poetry, can mean different things: the analogy
between music and poetry can be relatively subtle, as with Pater
and Verlaine, or it can be relatively crude, referring merely to the
sound-effects of rhythm, vowels and consonants. In practice, the
subtler form of the analogy – stressing rather the *effect* of poetry
than the means employed to gain it – also usually leads to a strong
interest in sound-effects. Thus another French Symbolist poet,
Arthur Rimbaud (1854–91) wrote a sonnet in which he sought to
convey the suggestive power of vowels by equating them with the
colours, black, white, red, green and blue:

> A noir, E blanc, I rouge, U vert, O bleu

The interest in sound-effects can evidently take a whimsical turn.
In this field, Poe came to be acknowledged as a pioneer. *The
Quarterly* commented in 1873:

> The word 'forlorn' which appeared so full of meaning to Keats, the
> word 'nevermore' which suggested to Edgar Poe the poem of 'The
> Raven' both exemplify the results that can be produced by the purely
> sensuous side of poetry. Nothing is more remarkable in modern
> English poetry than those curiosities of language and novelties of
> metre which attest the progress of this principle of composition.
>
> ('The State of English Poetry', July 1873)

The writer is obviously thinking of *The Philosophy of Composition*, where Poe describes how he wrote *The Raven*. This description shows a 'musical' concept of poetry in action.

Before describing the writing of *The Raven*, Poe declares his intention of showing 'that no one point in its composition is referable either to accident or intuition – that the work proceeded step by step, to its completion with the precision and rigid consequence of a mathematical problem'. Poe thus repudiates the idea that poets, in the process of composition, are carried away by a flow of 'inspiration', over which they have no conscious control: the poet is a conscious, calculating artist from first to last. Here Poe resembles Gautier and the French poets of the Parnassian school, who, rebelling against the emotionalism of Romantics such as De Musset, sought for control, impersonality, descriptive precision and perfection of form.

On his own account, Poe began to think about his projected poem with no subject in mind. His first consideration, he assures us, was merely that of extent: how long should the poem be? He decided on a length of approximately one hundred lines. The next consideration was 'the choice of an impression or effect to be conveyed'. The effect, as of any poem, should be one of Beauty; and, since Beauty, when most affecting, is touched with sadness, it followed that, for greatest effect, the tone should be one of melancholy.

Having decided on the length, the province (Beauty) and the tone (melancholy) of his poem, Poe used 'ordinary induction' to find an artistic device that would give it piquancy and point. He eventually decided on the refrain. Then he decided that the refrain should be a single word; but what sort of word? Musical considerations prevailed:

Having made up my mind to a *refrain*, the division of the poem into stanzas was of course a corollary, the *refrain* forming the close to each stanza. That such a close, to have force, must be sonorous and susceptible of protracted emphasis admitted no doubt, and these considerations inevitably led me to the long *o* as the most sonorous vowel in connection with *r* as the most producible consonant.

The word 'nevermore' immediately presented itself. All Poe now needed was a pretext for the continuous use of it. Deciding that a non-human speaker would be best, he first thought of a parrot, then decided that a raven would be more in keeping with the prevailing tone. He then had to devise a human situation in which a raven constantly repeating the word 'nevermore' would be particularly telling. A lover bewailing his dead mistress seemed appropriate. Eventually he wrote the stanza which became the third-from-last of the finished poem:

> 'Prophet!' said I, 'thing of evil! prophet
>   still if bird or devil!
> By that Heaven that bends above us – by that
>   God we both adore,
> Tell this soul with sorrow laden if, within
>   the distant Aidenn,
> It shall clasp a sainted maiden whom the angels
>   name Lenore —
> Clasp a rare and radiant maiden whom the angels
>   name Lenore.'
>   Quoth the raven – 'Nevermore'.

We may suspect Poe of rationalization: his account is certainly inspired by a desire to promote a particular doctrine about poets and poetry. Poets, he argues, are deliberate artists, not wild visionaries; and the achievement of 'Beauty', which is the true end of poetry, depends more on a mastery of form and music than on feeling. Subject-matter is of subordinate importance. The important thing is the 'Tone' – or, as we might say, the mood: the subject merely carries the mood – so that the poet, on Poe's showing, may first decide on the mood and then select a subject to fit it. In fact Poe represents himself as selecting his subject only in the final stages of the preliminary brainwork that went into *The Raven*;

he started with merely the bare intention of writing a poem. Instrumental music touches us by conveying a mood without reference to any situation in life; on Poe's view, poetry touches us in a comparable way, referring to a situation but subordinating it to a direct evocation of mood by the combined sounds and general associations of words. ('Nevermore' has, after all, some melancholy force independently of any particular context in which it may occur.) If we turn to *The Raven*, we find that its effect is heavily dependent on rhythm, repetition, internal rhyme and verbal texture.

Poe's doctrine would give subject-matter in *all* poetry the subordinate role that it usually has in a song. A song may, on occasion, have a particularly interesting lyric which commands attention in its own right; but this is obviously not necessary. And the effect of a musical setting is almost always to blur verbal attention in some degree. The effect of 'musical' technique, as in Poe and later poets such as Swinburne or Dylan Thomas, is to blur verbal awareness without the aid of a (literal) musical setting. Poe seems to regard music as the supreme art, and asserts, this time in *The Poetic Principle*, that poetry's most promising field of development is in conjunction with music. 'The old Bards and Minnesingers had advantages which we do not possess – and Thomas Moore, singing his own songs, was, in the most legitimate manner, perfecting them as poems.' The ideal poem is – literally – the song.

For Poe, Tennyson is 'the noblest poet that ever lived'; and he cites the lyric, 'Tears, idle tears . . .' from *The Princess* —

> Tears, idle tears, I know not what they mean,
> Tears from the depths of some divine despair —

as an example of true poetry. Tennyson is 'noble', not for any nobility of sentiment, but for his mastery of that musicality on which poetic Beauty depends.

*   *   *

Poe's ideas exerted a more important direct influence in France than they did in America and England. Baudelaire was fascinated by Poe's bizarre imagination and his anticipations of 'decadent' feeling. He was also sufficiently impressed by Poe's poetic theory to comment on it in his own essays; and it was through the influence of Baudelaire on his English devotee, Algernon Charles Swinburne, that Poe significantly affected the development of ideas of art for art's sake in England.

Swinburne first won acclaim for his *Atalanta in Calydon* (1865) in which his powers appeared already fully formed. *Poems and Ballads* (1866) evoked a different reception, celebrating, as they did, emotions commonly deemed reprehensible – masochistic sensuality, for instance, in *Dolores*, Lesbian passion in *Faustine*. The volume breathed a defiant neo-paganism, a hankering after the untroubled sensuality enjoyed in an idealized pagan antiquity. Inevitably there was a loud and hostile reaction which, as it gathered strength, embraced other poets, notably Rossetti, the principal target of Robert Buchanan's article, 'The Fleshly School of Poetry' (1871). Swinburne counter-attacked vigorously in *Notes on Poems and Reviews* (1866), fulminating against 'the prurient prudery and virulent virtue of pressmen and prostitutes'. When he came to publish his long essay, *William Blake* (1868), he devoted much of the second chapter to what is virtually the first unequivocal and sustained exposition in English of art for art's sake – though, at bottom, he was perhaps less concerned with theories of art than with vindicating the artist's (particularly his own) claim to freedom of expression. Despite his heavy reliance on formal effects, on the musical evocation of mood, the poet of *Poems and Ballads* is less an aesthete than a rebel. (His political revolutionary sympathies – witness *A Song of Italy* (1867) and *Songs before Sunrise* (1871) – were strong.) However, he was not a man for half-measures, and, choosing to espouse art for art's sake, he carried the attitude to extremes. He

E

was, it should be added, an admirer of Gautier as well as of Baudelaire.

He took as occasion his pioneering study of William Blake (1757-1827), poet, painter, engraver and visionary thinker, representing Blake as a votary of art for art's sake. For this interpretation he could plead some justification:

> A Poet, a Painter, a Musician, an Architect: the Man Or Woman who is not one of these is not a Christian.
> The Whole Business of Man is the Arts, and All Things in Common. No Secrecy in Art.

The above statements were added by Blake, in the later years of his life, to an engraving of the Laocoon. Years earlier, he had proclaimed that 'the Poetic Genius' is the source of true vision. To see life solely in terms of the detached, analytic reason, or of abstractly conceived and applied morality, is to divide and distort our humanity. 'If Morality was Christianity' – to quote again from the Laocoon engraving – 'Socrates was the Saviour'.

Like Swinburne, Blake detested the conventional morality of 'Thou shalt nots'. When, however, Swinburne represents him as an apostle of art for art's sake, we come up against the logical circularity of that formula. Two people may both value art 'for its own sake', while having such different views of art that it is virtually pointless to regard them as sharing the same doctrine. For Blake, art was more than a matter of beautiful effects: it embodied a vision of reality, and it was the vision that was supremely important. He would certainly have scorned any conventional Victorian view of art as an agency for inducing people to be model citizens. But Blake's belief in art is related to a comprehensive religious philosophy, however unorthodox. In art, we enter the eternal world of imagination, imagination being equated with reality. (Philosophically, Blake may be regarded as a sort of idealist, who talks of 'imagination' where a professional philosopher would talk of 'mind'.) Again, the aesthete stands for the separation of one human interest – the aesthetic – from others, such as the religious, the philosophical, the moral; but Blake stands for wholeness, the completeness of 'the Divine Humanity', in which all the powers of the human soul work together.

The contrast between Blake and the aesthetes enforces the point that 'art for art's sake', as proclaimed in the nineteenth century, implied this exclusive view of the aesthetic, as something discontinuous with the rest of life, and of art as properly concerned only with aesthetic effect. This is the view that Swinburne urges in *William Blake*. He recognizes the all-embracing character of Blake's vision, while also trying to align him with the aesthetic exclusiveness of his own day. Thus Blake is one to whom

> all faith, all virtue, all moral duty or religious necessity, was not so much abrogated or superseded as summed up, included and involved, by the one matter of art. To him, as to other such workmen, it seemed better to do this well and let all the rest drift than to do incomparably well in all other things and dispense with this one.

Swinburne will admit no compromise between the artist and the puritan; and the great men on either side never attempt to come to terms: 'Savonarola burnt Boccaccio; Cromwell proscribed Shakespeare. The early Christians were not great at verse or sculpture.' Swinburne does not seem to be aware of any morality other than a puritan-humanitarian one in which the good life consists solely in usefulness to others. To that extent, his outlook is as limited as that of his opponents who regard 'an earnest life or a great active poem (that is, material virtue or the mere doing and saying of good or instructive deeds and words) as infinitely preferable to any possible feat of art'. Swinburne has even a certain respect for the uncompromising puritan – who is at least clear-sighted in recognizing the irreconcilability of art and morality (or religion). His contempt is reserved for those who are ready 'with the consecrating hand, to lend meritorious art and poetry a timely pat or shove'. It is better to kill art outright than to cripple it by forcing it to perform a didactic function that is foreign to it. Whether Swinburne's view of art and morality is true or not, he seems, in his apparent inability to envisage more than one set of alternatives, to be hamstrung by the very puritan tradition he is trying to shake off.

He invokes Baudelaire on 'the great didactic heresy' (*l'hérésie de l'enseignement*), contending that the distinctive value of a work of art has nothing to do with instructiveness or beneficial moral effect. Art may in fact have moral effects, but these are incidental: the true artist does not make them his aim. Swinburne's position seems to become one of extreme formalism: what a poet actually says is in itself unimportant.

> Strip the sentiments and re-clothe them in bad verse, what residue will be left of the slightest importance to art? Invert them, retaining the manner or form (supposing this to be feasible, which it might be) and art has lost nothing.

'Form', then, is everything – but form, when it is freed from everything relating to meaning, amounts to very little. It would include metrical, rhyme and stanza schemes; patterns of alliteration and assonance; sentence-structure; rhythmical effects; and, perhaps, the associations which cling to some words, like 'nevermore' and 'forlorn', apart from context. It is natural to wonder if Swinburne was so little concerned with the meaning of his own poetry. Granted, his technique often inhibits too close an attention to meaning; but this, as we see in advertising and political propaganda, is quite consistent with a desire to put ideas across. In *William Blake*, his position is, in fact, strangely qualified in a footnote: 'it is assumed, to begin with, that the artist has something to say or do worth doing or saying in artistic form'. Swinburne thus reintroduces meaning by the back door. It seems reasonable to ask what criterion of worth is to be employed, and whether the qualification does not undermine his whole contention. Swinburne maintained his formalist position in later essays: one reviewer of his *Essays and Studies* (1875) not unreasonably suggested that, on such principles, Milton could have taken a broomstick as his subject and still written as great a poem as *Paradise Lost*.

* * *

While Swinburne was publishing *Poems and Ballads*, and the prose writings occasioned or influenced by the violent reaction to that volume, Walter Pater was publishing essays expounding contemplative aestheticism. These were on Coleridge; on the German eighteenth-century devotee of Greek art, Johann Joachim Winckelmann; and on the poetry of William Morris; they appeared, in the radical *Westminster Review*, in 1866, 1867 and 1868 respectively. The essay on Morris, later reprinted as 'Aesthetic Poetry', included a passage that became the conclusion of *The Renaissance*. Thus the two aspects of 'aesthetic' theory emerged, in unmistakable form, at the same time; though Pater did not evoke any widespread public response until *The Renaissance* came out in 1873.

Here we are concerned with Pater's ideas on matter and form in art. In his most important discussions of this subject, he maintains the second of the positions indicated in the first chapter: that, in our actual experience of works of art, 'form' and 'matter' are not clearly separable; and that the more difficult it is to see them apart, the better is the work of art. This is his contention in an essay on 'The School of Giorgione', where he makes the famous pronouncement that 'all art constantly aspires to the condition of music' – because in music we cannot, Pater believes, distinguish matter from form. Certainly, we cannot do it as we can in literature, or in representational graphic art. It follows for Pater, as for Poe, that the norm of excellence in poetry is lyric poetry which, 'precisely because in it we are least able to detach the matter from the form, without a deduction of something from that matter itself, is, at least artistically, the highest and most complete form of poetry'. ('At least artistically' is an interesting – if rather cryptic – qualification.) 'The perfection of lyric poetry', he goes on to say, often depends on 'a certain suppression or vagueness of mere subject.' The 'mere' might suggest a Swinburnian formalism; but Swinburne's position, as we remember, involves the assumption that it *is* possible sharply to separate the formal elements in poetry from its matter. Pater argues that because of the suppression of subject, the meaning of the poem cannot be sharply separated from the body of the poem; it 'reaches us through ways not distinctly traceable by the under-standing'; and he gives as examples 'some of the more imaginative compositions of William Blake' and the song, 'Take, oh take those lips away', from Shakespeare's *Measure for Measure*. Following Pater's hint, we may take one of Blake's lyrics, *The Sick Rose* from *Songs of Experience*, as an example of what he means:

> O Rose, thou art sick!
> The invisible worm
> That flies in the night,
> In the howling storm,
>
> Has found out thy bed
> Of crimson joy,
> And his dark secret love
> Does thy life destroy.

The 'vagueness' of the subject-matter here – if 'vague' is the word – results from the fact that it cannot be abstracted, without serious impoverishment, from the symbol in which it is conveyed. One could paraphrase the poem – as describing how corruption over-takes sexual love – but without ever being confident of having exhausted its suggestiveness. Blake concentrates a whole area of meaning in a vivid symbol. Pater notes the same effect of concen-tration when he says, of 'Take, oh take those lips away . . .', that in it 'the whole kindling force of the play seems to pass for a moment into an actual strain of music'. Another instance may be helpful – this time a late-medieval lyric, printed in *The Oxford Book of English Verse*, under the title, *Bridal Morning*:

> The maidens came
> When I was in my mother's bower;
>   I had all that I would.
>   The bailey beareth the bell away
>   The lily, the rose, the rose I lay.
>
> The silver is white, red is the gold;
> The robes they lay in fold.
>   The bailey beareth the lull away;
>   The lily, the rose, the rose I lay.
>
> And thro the glass window shines the sun.
> How should I love, and I so young?
>   The bailey beareth the lull away;
>   The lily, the rose, the rose I lay.

This poem poignantly expresses the feelings of a young girl on her wedding morning. But the feeling is almost completely merged in the sensuous effect of the poem, and reaches us largely through that effect. Only in one line is it made completely explicit.

Whether we agree that this is the ideal sort of poetry, we can at least see what Pater meant. His view resembles that of the French Symbolists, as expressed in Verlaine's *Art poétique*:

> De la musique avant toute chose,
> Et pour cela préfère l'Impair
> Plus vague et plus soluble dans l'air,
> Sans rien en lui qui pèse ou qui pose.
>
> Il faut aussi que tu n'ailles point
> Choisir tes mots sans quelque méprise:
> Rien de plus cher que la chanson grise
> Où l'Indécis au Précis se joint.

(Music before everything,
and for that prefer the Uneven – the Not-
   too-exactly–equivalent —
vaguer and more soluble in air,
with nothing in it that is heavy or stays
   at rest.

Also you must not set yourself
to choose your words without a certain
   obliqueness:
nothing more precious than the grey song
where the Indefinite is joined to the Precise.)

The poetry envisaged by Verlaine is 'vague' only because its range
of suggestion is not sharply limited. As in *The Sick Rose*, image
and symbol may still, in themselves, be sharply presented: 'where
the Indefinite is joined to the Precise.' Like Verlaine, Pater is not
regarding 'form' as purely extraneous to matter and imposed upon
it. Rather, a state of mind is conveyed directly by symbol and
image – as in music by a pattern of sound – rather than indirectly
by, for example, the detailed, explicit description of a human situation.

*   *   *

The final development, in English, of nineteenth-century views
of 'pure poetry' is perhaps represented by the Irish novelist,
George Moore (1852–1933) who in his later years published an
anthology with introduction – *Pure Poetry* (1924) – designed to
expound and illustrate his idea of what was and was not validly
poetic. With a scepticism recalling Pater (whom he had long
admired) Moore urges that only 'the world of things' is permanent.
Ideas constantly change and lose their force; but things remain.
Cowper's lines

> The poplars are fell'd; farewell to the shade,
> And the whispering sound of the cool colonnade

retain their freshness

> for there are always poplars in the world and men will always enjoy
> the whispering sound of a leafy avenue; but all that is essentially
> Cowper, his thoughts, his meditations, his ideas, have passed away,
> never to return. Wherefore the lines I have quoted do not undermine,
> rather do they uphold the belief that time cannot wither nor custom
> stale poetry unsicklied o'er with the pale cast of thought.

Modern poetry, says Moore, lacks 'innocency of vision', a quality
often derided as 'art for art's sake'. But what do people mean by
the phrase?

> It has been babbled for the last thirty or forty years, very few caring
> to ask themselves if art could be produced for other than aesthetic
> reasons, and the few that did fall to thinking do not seem to have dis-
> covered that art for art's sake means pure art, that is to say, a vision
> almost detached from the personality of the poet.

There is more poetry in things than in ideas: the poet should cut
out the buzzing of ideas in his own head, and be simply receptive to
the world of things. He praises Gautier's sonnet *La Tulipe*, in
which the poet extols the tulip's beauty of colour and shape – so
far Moore recalls the French Parnassians rather than the Symbolists
– and disparages Wordsworth's sonnet, *On Westminster Bridge*,
because it is tainted by Wordsworth's determination to see a soul
in the city, as well as in nature. The poem has 'a carefully concealed
morality in it'.

The rest of Moore's introduction consists of a faintly Wildean
dialogue between himself and the poets, John Freeman and Walter
de la Mare. The three discuss the contents of the projected anthology of 'objective poetry' – poetry which renders the world of
things with no intrusion of the poet's own ideas or even of
recognizably personal feeling. If we search Moore's anthology

for elucidation of this concept, we find that all of Blake's *Songs of Experience* – to which *The Sick Rose* belongs – are excluded, though *Songs of Innocence* are well represented. There are several poems by Coleridge and Shelley, none by Wordsworth and only one by Keats, who, in general, is too 'subjective'. Moore thus diverges from the view of Keats maintained by Pater and Wilde. This divergence points, I suggest, to two different, even incompatible interpretations of 'art for art's sake', which can conveniently be labelled the Romantic and the Parnassian. The first stresses self-expression, the right of the artist to express what he has it *in* him to express, and his artistic obligation to confine himself to that. The second interpretation stresses rather the work of art itself, as existing independently, even, of its creator; the aim of the true artist is not to express himself but to make something beautiful. We can thus admire a piece of pure poetry as we admire a Ming vase, for some 'objective' quality of beauty, without any thought of the man who made it. Thus Moore conceives of pure poetry as 'something that the poet creates outside of his own personality'. The idea that the poem should be considered independently of the poet, has enjoyed – though independently of Moore's advocacy – considerable currency in this century, in the prose writings of T. S. Eliot and among the 'new critics' in America.

* * *

In Moore, the idea of pure poetry reached an extreme which Pater did not envisage. In his criticism, Pater is strongly conscious of the man behind the work and of the personal vision embodied in it. (As when he says that Botticelli painted religious subjects 'with an under-current of original sentiment' – which it is the critic's business to isolate and define; or when, in his essay on Wordsworth, he mentions the 'inborn religious placidity' which informs Wordsworth's view of nature.) In his essay on 'Style' (1888), he declares, following Flaubert, that the style is the man: the criterion of good literary art is success in giving objective form to the writer's personal vision. In contrast to Moore who extols poetry in which 'things' are presented with no obscuring haze of subjectivity, Pater declares that the imaginative writer's aim is to give us 'not fact, but his peculiar sense of fact'.

> For just in proportion as the writer's aim, consciously or unconsciously, comes to be the transcribing, not of the world, not of mere fact, but of his sense of it, he becomes an artist, his work *fine* art; and good art (as I hope ultimately to show) in proportion to the truth of his presentment of that sense.

Thus the historian, for example, may become an artist in so far as his writing embodies not only fact, but sense of fact; and the criterion of 'good art' applies to all imaginative writing, whether in prose or verse. Style, then, is not merely a matter of 'form', in the narrowest sense of adornment, of something imposed on the subject-matter. It is something much more intimately related to the matter: without it, the artist's personal vision, his 'sense of fact' could not find objective embodiment. Echoing Flaubert's phrase, *le mot juste*, he declares that 'for every lineament of the vision within' there is 'the one acceptable word'. Pater had his own leanings towards euphuism, the cultivation of style in a merely decorative sense, but in this essay he repudiates it, invoking Flaubert whose search 'was not for the smooth, or winsome, or forcible word . . . but quite simply and honestly, for the word's adjustment to its meaning'.

In the artistic importance he attaches to import, to the artist's vision, Pater contrasts with Swinburne's formalism; in his emphasis on subjectivity, '*sense* of fact', he contrasts with Moore's emphasis on 'the world of things', and on objectivity. But his differences with both extend much further – to a point at which he discards the 'aesthetic' position completely. At the close of the essay, he offers a distinction between 'good art' and 'great art': great art does not only fulfil the condition of good art – which it must to be art at all; it also treats great human issues. As Pater says, greatness depends not on form but on matter.

> If it be devoted further to the increase of men's happiness, to the redemption of the oppressed, or the enlargement of our sympathies with each other, or to such presentment of new or old truth about ourselves and our relation to the world as may ennoble and fortify us in our sojourn here, or immediately, as with Dante, to the glory of God, it will also be great art.

There is some literature, then, that can properly be judged by moral, ethical and religious criteria. Pater could scarcely be departing further from anything that was currently understood by 'art for art's sake' – including his own earlier position as stated at the close of *The Renaissance*: there art promises 'nothing but the highest quality to your moments as they pass'. ('Highest' can scarcely refer to anything but intensity and subtlety of effect, since Pater's early scepticism rules out any wider scheme of values.) Pater had spoken of 'the limits within which art, undisturbed by any moral ambition, does its most sincere and surest work'. By contrast, his acceptance, almost twenty years later, of art 'devoted . . . to the redemption of the oppressed', is almost fulsome.

Apart from the conclusion of *The Renaissance*, Pater's early references to art for art's sake are fairly guarded – pointing mainly to the artistic dangers of conscious moral intention. He is never as forthright in dissociating art from morality as are Poe, Swinburne, Wilde and Moore. Also he recognizes, in an essay on *Measure for Measure* (1874), that, whether or not art is motivated by conscious moral intention, it may still have moral import. By leading us to enter imaginatively into situations, it may awake that 'finer knowledge through love' on which true justice towards others depends:

> It is not always that poetry can be the exponent of morality; but it is this aspect of morals which it represents most naturally, for this true

justice is dependent on just those finer appreciations which poetry cultivates in us the power of making, those peculiar valuations of action and its effect which poetry actually requires.

Here, even in the early Pater, we find an appreciation – all too rare in Victorian times – that literature may have a moral import, without being didactic in any explicit and direct way – without, that is, spelling out a 'moral' in the manner of a sermon or cautionary tale. Some other Victorians did, however, appreciate the point: George Eliot expressed it admirably in a letter, *à propos* of the suggestion that she should advocate social reforms in her novels.

My function is that of the aesthetic, not the doctrinal teacher, the rousing of the nobler emotions which make mankind desire the social right, not the prescribing of special measures, concerning which the artistic mind, however strongly moved by social sympathy, is often not the best judge.

The novelist or poet teaches by example not by precept; he should leave the reader to draw any practical conclusions. If this distinction between explicit and implicit moral import had been more commonly realized both by moralists and aesthetes, much contention between the two parties might have been avoided.

4
Exponents of
Aestheticism: Pater and Wilde

In the late sixties, both Swinburne and Pater voiced a spirit of revolt against puritan values and in favour of a mode of life that allowed freer play to the senses and a higher value to the arts and to beauty in its distinctively sensuous forms. Of the two, Pater had by far the milder temperament; and, after the charges of amoral hedonism evoked by *The Renaissance*, he withdrew the offending conclusion from the second edition, restoring it, in a slightly chastened form, in subsequent editions. In later years, he became more sympathetic to Christianity, finding in religious ritual the expression of a form of life that was at once refined and idealized and yet pleasing to the senses. In these pages, we shall be concerned, however, with the early essays in which he is most representative of the general movement of English aestheticism.

In his essay on Coleridge, Pater advanced a sceptical and relativist view of life: the advance of science, and of critical thought generally, is fostering 'the relative spirit'. Absolutes in ethics and religion are crumbling. Science represents man as part of nature and nature itself as a process of constant change. Ideas, values and beliefs are themselves the products of historical change; they reflect historical circumstances and, with the passing of those circumstances, must pass away themselves.

> The relative spirit has . . . started a new analysis of the relations of body and mind, good and evil, freedom and necessity. Hard and abstract moralities are yielding to a more exact notion of the subtlety and complexity of our life.

Morality becomes more flexible and humane: it allows for the peculiar needs and difficulties of individuals, recognizing that circumstances alter cases. Thus, in writing of Winckelmann, Pater defends that writer's homosexual attachments. Swinburne might have invoked 'the relative spirit' in defence of the deviant feeling in *Poems and Ballads*; and the process Pater describes has evidently continued apace since the eighteen-sixties: 'the new morality' and 'the sexual revolution', are developments that Pater virtually anticipates. Pater urges that, since 'the relative spirit' is eroding our belief in realities transcending experience, we shall be wise to make the most of experience itself, abandoning futile speculation.

> Who would change the colour or curve of a rose-leaf for that . . . colourless, formless, intangible, being . . . Plato put so high? For the true illustration of the speculative temper is . . . one such as Goethe, to whom every moment of life brought its contribution of experimental, individual knowledge; by whom no touch of the world of form, colour, and passion was disregarded.

The mention of Goethe recalls that the foreign influences on the early Pater were overwhelmingly not French but German: Goethe, Winckelmann, Lessing, Hegel, Heine.

Winckelmann interests Pater as one who intuitively sympathized with classical sculpture and thus recaptured the untroubled pagan acceptance of sensuous beauty. Pater's comments on this aspect of Winckelmann reveal the moral embarrassments which a Victorian aesthete had to contend with:

> Greek sensuousness . . . does not fever the conscience: it is shameless and childlike. Christian asceticism, on the other hand, discrediting the slightest touch of sense, has from time to time provoked into strong emphasis the contrast or antagonism to itself, of the artistic life, with its inevitable sensuousness. – *I did but taste a little honey with the end of the rod that was in mine hand, and lo! I must die.* – It has sometimes seemed hard to pursue that life without something of a disavowal of a

spiritual world; and this imparts to genuine artistic interests a kind of intoxication. From this intoxication Winckelmann is free; he fingers those pagan marbles with unsinged hands, with no sense of shame or loss.

Pater here recalls Swinburne's denunciation of Christianity:

Thou has conquered, O pale Galilean; the world has grown grey from thy breath.

More restrainedly, Pater bewails the Christian heritage of anxiety, and the impossibility of a simple enjoyment of sensuous beauty:

Plato . . . glances with a somewhat blithe and naive inconsequence from one view to another, not anticipating the burden of importance 'views' will one day have for men. In reading him one feels how lately it was that Croesus thought it a paradox to say that external prosperity was not necessarily happiness. But on Coleridge lies the whole weight of the sad reflection that has since come into the world, with which for us the air is full, which the 'children in the market place' repeat to each other.

Christianity has so conditioned our minds that for modern men 'the Greek spirit, with its engaging naturalness . . . is itself the Sangrail of an endless pilgrimage'. Meanwhile, the artist, whose soul tends to become 'more and more immersed in sense', is at odds with a puritan morality which spurns the senses and a religion which sets its sights on purely spiritual realities.

Closely connected with Pater's early neo-paganism is his interest in the Renaissance. In this interest he was not alone. Victorians who craved a livelier recognition of the arts and of sensuous beauty, could easily see Renaissance man – recovering the fire of pagan antiquity – as a mythic, Promethean figure. Swinburne, Pater and J. A. Symonds in his massive *Renaissance in Italy* (1875–86) all hold this somewhat simplified perspective of Western culture.

Pater's historicism distinguishes him from other, more extreme exponents of aestheticism. In his dialogue, 'The Decay of Lying', Oscar Wilde's own spokesman expressly denies that 'art expresses the temper of its age, the spirit of its time, the moral and social conditions that surround it, and under whose influence it is produced'. Art 'rejects the burden of the human spirit. . . . She is not symbolic of any age'. In *The Renaissance*, however, Pater quite explicitly regards art and literature as reflecting 'that complex, many-sided movement' – as in his famous comment on the Mona Lisa:

> All the thoughts and experience of the world have etched and moulded there, in that which they have of power to refine and make expressive the outward form, the animalism of Greece, the lust of Rome, the mysticism of the middle age with its spiritual ambition and imaginative loves, the return of the Pagan world, the sins of the Borgias.

Art, as much as any other product of the human mind, is to be seen 'relatively and under conditions'. Thus he holds that 'painting, music, and poetry, with their endless power of complexity, are the special arts of the romantic and modern ages'. The arts have to deal with the experience with which the age provides them: that experience is nowadays immensely complex, and only those arts can deal with it that are capable of a corresponding complexity of treatment. Pater differs, then, from Wilde, in 'The Decay of Lying', and those 'new critics' of the present century who repudiate any concern either with the man who created the work or with the historical conditions that influenced him. However, Pater's view of historical conditions, in *The Renaissance* and the essay on Coleridge, is somewhat rarified: he is aware of philosophical, ethical, religious influences; but he disregards social, political and economic factors. His view, both of past and present, reflects his dominant pre-occupation with the cultivation of the mind, with 'self-culture'.

Pater's version of 'self-culture' is focused on the present moment:

F

A counted number of pulses only is given to us of a variegated, dramatic life. How may we see in them all that is to be seen in them by the finest senses? How shall we pass most swiftly from point to point, and be present always at the focus where the greatest number of vital forces unite in their purest energy?

The aim is to preserve a state of self-possessed awareness in which the distinctiveness and novelty of specific experiences are keenly perceived; for 'it is only the roughness of the eye that makes any two persons, things, situations seem alike'. Life must be 'variegated and dramatic'; we must bring to it 'a quickened, multiplied consciousness'. Pater's idea of being 'present . . . where the greatest number of vital forces unite' recalls Goethe's ideal of life in the whole – '*im Ganzen*' – an ideal to which Pater elsewhere gives his characteristic twist:

> Every one who aims at the life of culture is met by many forms of it. . . . But the pure instinct of self-culture cares not so much to reap all that those various forms of genius can give, as to find in them its own strength. The demand of the intellect is to feel itself alive. . . . It struggles with those forms till its secret is won from each, and then lets each fall back into its place, in the supreme, artistic view of life.

Thus the service of philosophy is to rouse and startle us to 'a life of constant and eager observation'. Everything returns in the end to the self, the individual mind: a philosophy is valuable, not for its truth, but for its capacity to stir and enliven our perceptions of the life around us.

Pater's 'supreme artistic view of life', like Arnold's 'Culture', owes much to Goethe who, more than any other writer, was the inspiration of Victorian English ideas of self-culture. Goethe's ideal involves roundedness, centrality, and also detachment; both these aspects appear in Arnold. Pater gives them a peculiarly subjective slant. Centrality is the centrality of the self, of a subjective, aesthetic viewpoint.

For all his scepticism, however, Pater evinces an incongruous hankering for some rarified ideal existence transcending the ordinary human lot. Temperamentally at least, he had his Platonist side. Thus he describes a scene in a frieze from the Parthenon – a 'line of youths on horseback, with their level glances, their proud, patient lips, their chastened reins, their whole bodies in exquisite service'. In this scene Pater finds a 'colourless, unclassified purity of life' that is 'the highest expression of the indifference which lies beyond all that is relative or partial'.

Ideals of life caught Pater's imagination only as embodied in some beautiful form – in art or ritual or attractive persons. Pater was an Oxford don and, when asked by a student: 'Why should we be moral?', is said to have replied: 'Because it is so beautiful.' The reply may fall feebly on twentieth-century ears; Plato, however, would, at least partly, have agreed with it.

*   *   *

By the late seventies, aestheticism was gaining ground, notably in the artistic theories of the American painter, James Macneil Whistler (1834–1903). Whistler scorned the narrative painting popular at the time and insisted that it was not the subject that was important in painting – not even if it was your own mother – but composition, the arrangement of colours, forms, light and shade. Painting in this spirit and exhibiting at the Grosvenor Gallery – the abode, according to Gilbert, of the 'greenery-yallery' in art – he was abusively attacked by Ruskin, whom he sued for libel in 1878. The Whistler–Ruskin case shows the confrontation between naturalism – the idea that a work of art should meticulously reproduce the visible surface of things – and the idea that it is validated rather by its coherence as a composition. In his rejection of 'realism', Whistler carried 'art for art's sake' to a point at which Wilde took it up. For Wilde, realism, as much as moralism, is the foe of art. Whistler also anticipates Wilde in his conviction that art is for the minority: in his famous 'Ten O'Clock' lecture (1885) he even expresses two-edged sympathy for the art-afflicted public:

> The Dilettante stalks abroad. The amateur is loosed. The voice of the aesthete is heard in the land, and catastrophe is upon us.

Here Whistler is probably venting irritation with Wilde who had been giving popular lectures without any qualms about representing other men's ideas – including Whistler's – as his own. Like some other artistic practitioners, Whistler resented the amateur as incompetent and parasitic. Believing that art is for the few, he deplored Wilde's tendency to exploit artistic interests for public effect. Later, however, Wilde was to recall Whistler's pessimism, speaking of 'the great Darwinian principle of the survival of the vulgarest'.

Wilde settled in London in 1879. His whole career can be plausibly regarded as a search for identity, leading him first into an aesthetic pose, then, without his dropping the aesthetic attitudes, into a sophisticated, socialite pose. (Sir Henry Wotton in *Dorian Gray*, or the principal figures in the critical dialogues.) But Wilde is never sure that he has found the identity he seeks – or that there is any identity to find. Hence his pre-occupation with masks and the nonentity they conceal:

> Where we differ from each other is purely in accidentals: in dress, manner, tone of voice, religious opinions, personal appearance, tricks of habit and the like. The more one analyses people, the more all reasons for analysis disappear.

In Wilde's presentation, aestheticism becomes a cult of artificiality. 'The first duty in life is to be as artificial as possible. What the second duty is no one has as yet discovered.' We may escape from the banality of life by perfecting our mask, by finding a role and acting it to perfection. Contemplative aestheticism is flippantly transformed into histrionic aestheticism – into what a writer of the nineties, Richard Le Gallienne, was to term 'the dramatic art of life'.

Wilde's version of art for art's sake is defined by his opposition to three contemporary attitudes: realism; utilitarian moralism; and the idea of art as self-expression. Against the realist, he asserts that, so far from imitating life, art must improve on it. Against the moralist, he asserts that 'all art is perfectly useless', and that, in any case, the world is not likely to be improved by moral propaganda. Against the idea that we are to look in art for the meaning intended by the artist, he retorts that 'the meaning of any beautiful thing is, at least, as much in the soul of him who looks at it, as it was in his soul who wrought it'. Nor will any amount of feeling avail the artist without artistic skill. 'All bad poetry springs from genuine feeling.' Art does not exist to express the spirit of the age, or the eternal verities, or even the soul of its creator. 'Art never expresses anything but itself.'

Wilde advances his views on art mainly in the essays published, in volume form, in *Intentions* (1891): 'The Decay of Lying', 'Pen, Pencil and Poison', 'The Critic as Artist' and 'The Truth of Masks'. The first and third of these are in a dialogue form which gives added scope for flippancy: the main participant is a persona, a serio-comic mask which Wilde can hold to his face or let slip at will. The argument proceeds by hyperbole, paradox and calculatedly outrageous contentions. In the event, most readers are probably content to be entertained. But the comedian is, notoriously, often a sad man; and Wilde's pre-occupation with the banality of life represents more than a comic pose. Wilde's dread of banality led him strongly to emphasize the idealizing aspect of art. In 'The Critic as Artist', Ernest – the 'stooge' in the dialogue, not Wilde's persona – remarks that we should soon be wearied of the world if art did not 'purify it for us, and give to it a momentary perfection'. In 'The Decay of Lying', we read that Emile Zola, the great exponent of Realism, is aesthetically criminal in describing life exactly as it is. With some reason, Wilde urges that unless the contemporary reverence for facts is checked, 'Art will become sterile, and beauty will pass away from the land.' But his disparagement of 'Life' can go beyond such arguments:

> For when one looks back upon the life that was so vivid in its emotional intensity, and filled with such fervent moments of ecstasy or of joy, it all seems to be a dream and an illusion. What are the unreal things, but the passions that once burned one like fire? What are the incredible things, but the things that one has faithfully believed? What are the improbable things? The things that one has done oneself. No, Ernest; life cheats us with shadows, like a puppet-master.

This is as near the true voice of feeling as 'The Critic as Artist' ever gets: the world is *maya*, illusion. From this banal illusion we turn to the more vivid and reliable world of literature:

> The pain of Leopardi crying out against life becomes our pain. Theocritus blows on his pipe, and we laugh with the lips of nymph and shepherd. In the wolfskin of Pierre Vidal we flee before the hounds, and in the armour of Lancelot we ride from the bower of the Queen.

And so on. Such evocative commentary has no logical end. Wilde's argument leads to a parodox: Life imitates Art, not the other way round. Young ladies ape the style of beauty found in the paintings of Rossetti and Burne-Jones. 'The nineteenth century, as we know it, is largely an invention of Balzac.'

Wilde disparages not only Life but Nature too. A sunset is found to be 'a very second-rate Turner, a Turner of a bad period, with all the painter's worst faults exaggerated and overemphasized'. Nature exhibits an 'absolutely unfinished condition. Nature has good intentions, of course, but, as Aristotle once said, she cannot carry them out.' Under the persiflage, Wilde is attacking representationalism in art. As an undergraduate, he had been briefly a devotee of Ruskin; but here he is against Ruskin and with Whistler.

Wilde's case against moralistic views of art rests on the familiar ground that 'art finds her own perfection within, and not outside of, herself'. Therefore, to turn it to utilitarian and moral ends is to pervert it. 'The only beautiful things are the things that do not concern us' – that have no practical purpose. 'All art is perfectly useless.' He also flaunts a certain amoralism – as in 'Pen, Pencil and Poison', an essay on the early-nineteenth-century writer, painter, poisoner and forger, Thomas Griffiths Wainwright, in which Wilde makes the sensible point that 'the fact of a man being a poisoner is nothing against his prose'. His amoralism also takes the form of scepticism about the efficacy of human action, the reality of free will and the practical value of lofty intentions. 'It is well for his peace that the saint goes to his martyrdom. He is spared the sight of the horror of his harvest.'

For Wilde, art is not self-expression, not a mere outpouring of feeling. 'All fine imaginative work is self-conscious and deliberate.' Although art may inspire us, it does not itself spring from inspiration. In this, he represents the 'Parnassian' side of aestheticism, and strongly recalls Poe, stressing form rather than feeling.

> For the real artist is he who proceeds, not from feeling to form, but from form to thought and passion. He does not first conceive an idea, and then say to himself, 'I will put my idea into a complex metre of fourteen lines,' but, realizing the beauty of the sonnet-scheme, he conceives certain modes of music and methods of rhyme, and the mere form suggests what is to fill it and make it intellectually and emotionally complete.

This, of course, is precisely the process described by Poe in his account of the composition of *The Raven*. Both Wilde and Pater evince a certain reaction, if not against Romanticism, certainly against an excessive reliance on 'inspiration' or the force of feeling. Thus Pater, indebted as he is to Coleridge, expresses misgivings lest Coleridge's 'organic' view of literature should suggest that the creative process is blind and involuntary. (Coleridge himself always recognized the element of conscious will in poetic composition.) Pater's account of artistic creation is different from Wilde's: 'By exquisite analysis the artist achieves clearness of idea; then, through many stages of refining, clearness of expression.' But even though Pater gives importance to the 'idea', he insists just as much as Wilde on conscious artistry.

This insistence indicates that, in England as in France, aestheticism had its Parnassian aspect. Pater and Wilde, in upholding technique, conscious artistry, set themselves against any simple faith in 'inspiration' or spontaneous expression: for Wilde, as later for Moore, it is the poet's business not to unburden his soul but to make something beautiful. In France the situation had been even more clear-cut: Gautier, and the Parnassians after him, had deliberately upheld clarity of description and definiteness of form against the effusiveness of de Musset and his generation. In English aestheticism, however, there is a certain ambivalence: whereas Pater's theory of art is distinctly an expressive one, Wilde, following Poe, regards 'form' as exclusively important: what motivates the artist is his sense of form, not an idea of something he wants to convey. Wilde is thus taking up a more extreme, more unambiguously 'aesthetic' stance than Pater; and Pater's distinction between 'good art' and 'great art' is one for which Wilde's position gives no scope.

On the subject of criticism, Wilde takes the line that 'the highest Criticism deals with art not as expressive but as impressive purely' – that is, it concerns itself with the impression made upon the critic, not with interpreting the mind of the artist. From this he proceeds to the position that criticism is not concerned with saying anything about the work of art in itself: it merely takes the work as the starting-point for a second creation. Thus the problem raised by 'impressionist' or appreciative criticism – how to ensure that the critic's impressions are more than merely subjective – is dismissed: criticism is a form of art and, as such, it 'never expresses anything but itself'. When Pater tells us that the Mona Lisa 'is older than the rocks among which she sits', he tells us nothing about Leonardo's painting; but that does not matter – he has written an original prose-poem. Criticism is simply art at its furthest remove from life: art taking its material from art.

Wilde's view of the relation of life and art reflects his pessimism. Truth and substance are denied us: all we can achieve is effect, art itself being a matter of effect. Effects can at least be *felt*, and, if felt, they are incontestable; whereas the great abstractions – Truth and Morality – are elusive and debatable. Artistic values are thus more 'real' than those which conventional Victorians set above them. Wilde's viewpoint – if the above be a fair rendering of it – bears evident resemblances to Pater's. However, whereas Pater felt the splendour of experience, as well as its 'awful brevity', Wilde constantly harks back to its banality. Art, he claims, offers a refuge from banality. We may wonder, however, how long even art can retain its interest when the world at large is seen as inane and meaningless.

Conclusion

Aestheticism is often associated chiefly with the nineties, the period of Aubrey Beardsley and *The Yellow Book*. The tendency of aestheticism in the nineties was increasingly histrionic – towards a cult of dandyism, of deliberate mannerism in life and art. Earlier aesthetic and Pre-Raphaelite influences persisted, as in *The Yellow Book* itself, a hard-back periodical that began to appear in 1894, and reflected in its format the renaissance of artistic book-production most memorably evidenced in William Morris's Kelmscott Press, founded in 1891. It appealed to a modish taste for the new and the off-beat, though it also printed more conservative work. It acquired a popular reputation for 'decadent' perversity, which Beardsley's work as art-editor probably did nothing to dissipate. In the panic following Wilde's trial in 1895, Beardsley was, however, dismissed.

Practical aestheticism flourished in much of the verse of the time – in which Pater noted, 'amid an admirable achievement of poetic form, a certain lack of poetic matter'. Aesthetic dandyism flourished in the prose of Max Beerbohm – in, for instance, his *Yellow Book* essay, 'A Defence of Cosmetics'. Among less well-remembered authors may be mentioned Richard Le Gallienne, in essays like 'The Boom in Yellow' – on the fashionable taste for that colour – and 'The Dramatic Art of Life'. But aestheticism was losing its earlier intensity. Beerbohm recalled the intense eighties with mild amusement: 'Beauty had existed long before 1880. It was Oscar Wilde who managed her debut.' Wilde and Whistler, in defiance of conventional earnestness, had introduced a note of flippancy; and Beerbohm and Le Gallienne, in the essays cited, wrote largely with an eye to humorous effect. No one could interpret them as offering, like Pater, a seriously intended answer to the familiar Victorian question: 'How to live?' As the present century approached, the social and intellectual climate grew less favourable to aestheticism. The nineties hankered after novelty – these were the years of 'the New Woman', 'the New Hedonism', 'the New' generally – and aesthetic ideas were no longer novel. Also, social and political interests were reasserting their hold over the educated imagination. Morris had long been an apostle of socialism; even Wilde had flirted with it. Writers like Shaw, Wells and Chesterton were to evince, in differing ways, a new social hopefulness and a corresponding revulsion against aestheticism.

The development of 'aesthetic' ideas in England had not, however, simply come to a dead end. An outlook akin to that of nineteenth-century aestheticism persisted in the Bloomsbury circle in the early twentieth century; and one of its leading spirits, the art critic, Roger Fry (1866–1934) was already active in the nineties. Fry, springing from a famous Quaker family, was no mere urbane dilettante, but felt a serious concern with the question: what should be the place of art in our scheme of life? I shall conclude by citing a passage from his 'Essay on Aesthetics', in which he discusses the familiar 'aesthetic' topic of art and life, but pursues it to a point at which the term, 'aestheticism' becomes inadequate:

The artist might if he chose take a mystical attitude, and declare that the fulness and completeness of the imaginative life he leads may correspond to an existence more real and more important than any that we know of in mortal life. And in saying this, his appeal would find a sympathetic echo in most minds, for most people would, I think, say that the pleasures derived from art were of an altogether different character and more fundamental than merely sensual pleasures, that they did exercise some faculties which are felt to belong to whatever part of us there may be which is not entirely ephemeral and material.

Fry goes on to suggest that, as mankind comes to recognize the imaginative life as 'the completest expression of its own nature', actual life will come to be justified by its approximation to the imaginative life – not the other way round.

If Fry recalls Wilde, he also recalls Blake. The value of art is that it is an assertion of spirit: in it we discover our capacity for a life that is more than merely 'ephemeral and material'. Or, as Blake might have put it in his still more visionary idiom, we enter the eternal world of imagination. Applied to literature – Fry himself was concerned largely with painting – his view does not, as far as I can see, preclude extra-aesthetic criteria of 'depth' and 'serious-ness'. Fry's essential point is also independent of the particular idiom that he uses: the point that literature and the arts are valuable as evidencing and expressing our 'spiritual', supra-material capa-cities, not for any ulterior – and probably unverifiable – effects on conduct. I offer, finally, the suggestion that here is to be found one important element of truth in ideas of art for art's sake.

Bibliography

RELEVANT WRITERS

(a) *Victorian*

MORRIS, WILLIAM, *Hopes and Fears for Art: Five Lectures*, London, 1882.

For Morris's general outlook. Cf. *Selections* below.

The Earthly Paradise, 3 vols., London, 1868–70.

Note the introductory Apology – a frank expression of literary 'escapism'.

Selections from the Prose Works, ed. A. H. R. Ball, Cambridge, 1931.

PATER, WALTER, *The Renaissance: Studies in Art and Poetry*, Third edition, London, 1888.

Particularly the Preface, the Conclusion, 'Winckelmann' and 'The School of Giorgione'.

Appreciations, London, 1889.

First edition, containing 'Aesthetic Poetry', as well as 'Style' and 'Coleridge'. 'Aesthetic Poetry' appears in *Selected Works* below.

Marius the Epicurean, 2 vols., 1885.

Chapter IX ('New Cyrenaicism') contains Pater's maturer view of contemplative aestheticism.

Walter Pater: Selected Works, ed. Richard Aldington, London, 1948.

Works, ed. C. L. Shadwell, 10 vols., London, 1910–11.

ROSSETTI, D. G., 'Hand and Soul'.

See p. 45. Originally appeared in *The Germ*, I, December 1850. Now included in collected editions of his poems.

SWINBURNE, A. C., *William Blake*, London, 1868.
   See pp. 59–63 above.
   Poems and Ballads, London, 1866.
   Particularly *Dolores, Faustine* and *Hymn to Proserpine*.
   Complete Works (Bonchurch edition) 20 vols., 1925–7.

WHISTLER, J. M., *The Gentle Art of Making Enemies*, London,
1890.
   Particularly the 'Ten O'Clock' lecture.

WILDE, OSCAR, *Intentions*, London, 1891.
   See pp. 79–83 above.
   The Soul of Man under Socialism, London, 1895. (*Fortnightly
Review*, 1890.)
   Important for a just and comprehensive view of Wilde.
   The Works of Oscar Wilde, ed. G. F. Maine, London, 1948.
   Not complete, but adequate for the general student.

(b) *Post-Victorian*

BELL, CLIVE, *Art*, New Edition, London, 1949. (First edition,
1914.)
   Like Fry below, develops nineteenth-century lines of thought
on graphic art in fresh ways.

FRY, ROGER, *Vision and Design*, London, 1920.
   Particularly 'Art and Life' and 'An Essay on Aesthetics'.

MOORE, GEORGE, *Pure Poetry: an Anthology*, London, 1924.
   See pp. 66–68 above.

(c) *Foreign*

BAUDELAIRE, CHARLES, *Baudelaire on Poe: Critical Papers*,
trans. and ed. Lois Hyslop and Francis E. Hyslop Jr., Caroll-
town, 1952.
   With reference especially to Chapter 3 above.

GAUTIER, THÉOPHILE, *Mademoiselle de Maupin*, Paris, 1835.

Preface contains Gautier's ideas; novel exemplifies 'decadent' and 'aesthetic' sentiment.

HUYSMANNS, J. K., *A Rebours*, Paris, 1884.
See p. 22 above. Available in Penguin (*Against Nature*).

POE EDGAR ALLAN, *Works*, ed. John H. Ingram, 4 vols., London, 1899.
Volume Three contains essays mentioned pp. 50–58 above.

GENERAL AND BACKGROUND STUDIES

(a) *Aestheticism and related subjects*

ALDINGTON RICHARD (ed.), *The Religion of Beauty: Selections from the Aesthetes*, London, 1950.

GAUNT, WILLIAM, *The Aesthetic Adventure*, London, 1945.
Available in Pelican Books. Slanted towards the 'colourful'; but informative and highly readable.

JACKSON, HOLBROOK, *The Eighteen Nineties*, London, 1913.
A broad literary survey.

LEHMANN, A. G., *The Symbolist Aesthetic in France, 1885–95*, Oxford, 1950.
Particularly relevant to Chapter 3 above.

PRAZ, MARIO, *The Romantic Agony*, trans. Angus Davidson, London, 1933.
Surveys 'decadent' and psychologically deviant elements in nineteenth-century literature.

ROSENBLATT, LOUISE, *L'idée de l'art pour l'art dans la littérature anglaise pendant la période victorienne*, Paris, 1931.
Traces the emergence of 'aesthetic' ideas – more fully, unfortunately, than any writer in English.

WELLAND, D. R., *The Pre-Raphaelites in Literature and Art*, London, 1953.

Useful anthology with introduction.

WELLEK, RENÉ, *History of Modern Criticism, 1750–1950*, 4 vols., London, 1955–66.
Volumes Three and Four particularly relevant.

WIMSATT, WILLIAM K., JR. & BROOKS, CLEANTH, *Literary Criticism: a Short History*, New York, 1957.
Mainly Chapter 22, on 'art for art's sake'.

(b) *Romantic antecedents*

ABRAMS, M. H., *The Mirror and the Lamp: Romantic Theory and the Critical Tradition*, New York, 1953.
Brilliant, but fairly exacting, study of the emergence of Romantic attitudes.

QUINCEY, THOMAS DE, 'On Murder Considered as One of the Fine Arts'.
Appeared in *Blackwood's Magazine*, February 1827.
Printed in World's Classics *Selected English Essays*. Whimsically anticipates art for art's sake.

FORD, G. H., *Keats and the Victorians: a Study of his Influence and Rise to Fame*, New Haven, 1944.
Illuminates Keats's 'aesthetic' affinities.

HALLAM, A. H., 'On Some Characteristics of Modern Poetry, and on the Lyrical Poems of Alfred Tennyson'. Appeared in the *Englishman's Magazine*, August 1831; reprinted in J. D. Jump (ed.), *Tennyson: The Critical Heritage*, London, 1967.
Anticipates art for art's sake, the idea of 'appreciative' criticism, etc.

LAMB, CHARLES, *Essays of Elia*, London, 1823.
'On the Artificial Comedy of the Last Century' mentioned p. 13 above. Hints of contemplative aestheticism in e.g. 'A Complaint of the Decay of Beggars in the Metropolis'.

(c) *Anti-aesthetic satire*

GILBERT, W. S., *Patience; or Bunthorne's Bride,* first produced London, 1881.
v. *Complete Plays of Gilbert and Sullivan,* New York, 1936.
Savoy Operas, St Martin's Library Edition, London, 1957.
Shrewd, if Philistine caricature.

HITCHENS, ROBERT, *The Green Carnation,* London, 1894.
An amusing novel directed against Wilde.

Punch; or the London Charivari, London, 1841–.
Particularly volumes LXIX–LXXXVIII (1875–85).
These include Du Maurier's best anti-aesthetic cartoons.

(d) *Biographical and critical works*

BENSON, A. C., *Walter Pater,* London, 1906.
Biographical-cum-critical.

BUCKLEY, J. H., *Tennyson: the Growth of a Poet,* Cambridge, Mass., 1960.
With reference to pp. 25–27 above.

DOUGHTY, OSWALD, *Victorian Romantic: Dante Gabriel Rossetti,* London, 1949.
Standard study of Rossetti's career. Cf. Fleming below.

FLEMING, G. H., *Rossetti and the Pre-Raphaelite Brotherhood,* London, 1967.
With reference to pp. 43–47 above. Complements Doughty.

FLETCHER, IAN, *Walter Pater,* British Council, Writers and their Work Series, London, 1959.
Interesting short study with bibliography.

HOUGH, GRAHAM, *The Last Romantics,* London, 1949.
Studies of Ruskin, Rossetti, Pater among others.

LAFOURCADE, GEORGES, *Swinburne: a Literary Biography,* London, 1932.

The first detached and 'modern' biography.

LEAVIS, F. R., *New Bearings in English Poetry*, London, 1932.
First chapter gives a hostile view of the relevant tendencies in Victorian poetry. Cf. pp. 23–28 above.
Revaluation, London, 1936.
For Chapter VII, on Keats. Considers his 'aesthetic' affinities.

PEARSON, HESKETH, *Life of Oscar Wilde*, London, 1946.
Not the most solid biography of Wilde, but highly readable.

ROBSON, W. W., 'Pre-Raphaelite Poetry', in *From Dickens to Hardy*, Pelican Guide to English Literature, Vol. 6, Harmondsworth, 1958.
Reprinted as 'Three Victorian Poets', *Critical Essays*, London, 1966.
A sensitive application of 'Leavisite' principles to D. G. Rossetti, Christina Rossetti and Morris.

Index

Index